THE AMERICAN REVOLUTION

A CONCISE HISTORY FROM COLONIAL REBELLION TO THE WAR FOR INDEPENDENCE TO THE CONSTITUTION

ERIC PORTERFIELD

The American Revolution

A Concise History from Colonial Rebellion to the War for Independence to the Constitution

Eric Porterfield

❀ Created with Vellum

CONTENTS

INTRODUCTION

SEEDS OF DISCONTENT

"Four score and seven years ago our fathers brought forth on this continent, a new nation, conceived in Liberty, and dedicated to the proposition that all men are created equal."

— ABRAHAM LINCOLN, THE GETTYSBURG
ADDRESS (1863), HONORING UNION SOLDIERS
AFTER THE CIVIL WAR BATTLE OF
GETTYSBURG, PENNSYLVANIA.

The founding of these United States as a constitutional republic was one of the great breakthroughs of human history. The Ancient Greeks had tried a different type of government called, "democracy," and failed miserably. Various forms of tyranny had been the norm throughout the past, and ordinary people with power could be every bit as despotic. In their *Declaration of Independence,* America's Founding Fathers chose their words carefully, especially those first three words which spoke of the identity of those who confronted the abusive and arbitrary British government—"We the people..."

America's Founding Fathers not only knew history, but also retained a deep understanding of philosophy; they understood the pros and the cons of various approaches to society's problems. Those founders strove to achieve something uniquely different—something which would address the weaknesses of every other system which had come before.

In the century preceding the American Revolution, England experienced a fair amount of political upheaval. Catholic King James II of England was deposed by his daughter, Mary II and her husband, William III of Orange (the Netherlands). During this period English philosopher John Locke (1632–1704) wrote what is perhaps one of the greatest works of the Age of Enlightenment—*Two Treatises of Government*, published not long after his return to England. Locke decried the behavior of King James II who had suspended the parliaments of both England and Scotland, subsequently ruling by arbitrary decree. John Locke had the rather unique and radical viewpoint that all creatures born of the same species should be equal and "without subordination or subjection." By this he was arguing that both king and commoner were equal under God. He also suggested that freedom pre-exists government; man starts with freedom and only later acquires a need for government. And Locke believed that government exists to protect the rights of the individual—defending both freedom and lawfully acquired property. According to Locke, the purpose of law is not to eliminate or restrain freedom, but to safeguard and increase that freedom.

The concerns of Englishmen on keeping hard won liberties is a theme which ran through the popular culture of the late 17th century and into the 18th. The writings of John Locke greatly influenced one Thomas Jefferson across the Atlantic Ocean.

In that age, some two and a half centuries before today, the states were semi-sovereign and separate nations subservient only to England and to its king. They jealously guarded what autonomy they had. In fact, it seemed quite common for the citizens of this young nation, at least before the Civil War, to refer to their country in the plural—*these* United States; after the war between the North and South, it was more common to use the singular—*the* United States. This may seem to be a subtle change of little consequence, but it reveals a shift away from the viewpoints of America's founders, and away from the principles which sought to diffuse power in all its forms.

Throughout most of English history, the nation did not have or require a large, standing army because the nation was on an island. It relied more heavily on its navy. That large and powerful navy could not be used to tyrannize citizens as armies had been used in other nations all through history. The landed aristocracy in England wielded a great deal of power and guarded the decentralization of power more than any other monarchy. Thus, the philosophical basis of government in England, and later Great Britain, valued checks and balances against the whims of despotic leaders.

Because of Great Britain's growing empire throughout the 17th and 18th centuries, the once naval nation began to rely more heavily on large, standing armies to control their many colonies. Thus, the arbitrary nature of some parliamentary laws ran contrary to the spirit of English culture of the previous 500 years.

This book aims to explore the mindsets of those brave, colonial Englishmen and to understand why they decided to divorce themselves from that motherland across the sea.

While we investigate their concerns, we will also seek out inspiration of uncommon valor and creativity amongst those pioneers who had established homes in what has been called the New World.

No time in history has ever been perfect. No individual has ever been flawless. While America's founding was imperfect and based on dark compromises struck, when compared to the remainder of all human history, the founding of America was, unquestionably, the brightest change within the collective memory of our species.

THE SEEDS OF REVOLUTION

England had been a special nation for half a millennium, with many benefits not enjoyed by other countries. The *Magna Carta* (AD 1215) had established rights for others besides the king. No longer could the monarch abuse others at his own whim. The establishment of a bicameral Parliament in 1341 had created a separation of powers which helped to ameliorate the abuses found so often in governments of the past. Such tyranny returned only briefly under King James II of England in 1685, when, for three years, he ruled England and Scotland without the help or interference of Parliament.

While Englishmen on the home island enjoyed the liberties established in English common law, those who lived in the colonies had come to feel increasingly that they were little more than servants of the empire. English law did not protect them and they had no voice in government. The law as applied in the American colonies became ever more *ad hoc* in nature.

The homeland continued to take and take and take, but gave little or nothing in return. More and more, the colonials found it difficult to live their own lives and to enjoy the fruits of their own labor.

Over the previous four centuries, a great deal had changed in human societies. Besides the physical discovery of the Americas, natural philosophers—what we, today, call "scientists"—discovered that humility to empirical evidence provided far more meaningful rewards. Instead of doing as the Greeks had done—using superior intellect to deduce what nature must be like and then developing science around their own cleverness—the early Renaissance natural philosophers found that they needed to look and listen to what nature had to tell them. No matter how brilliant the individual scientist, their lack of infinite knowledge severely handicapped their ability to understand what nature already knew.

In this age of increasing humility and openness to all manner of discovery, civilization was blossoming in ways which the Ancient Greeks and Romans could never have imagined. Thus, the 18th century in Western Europe and Eastern America proved to be a collision between the old and the new—between selfish tyranny over fearful subjects and the new liberty of ideas, discovery, and humility to God. America's founders were a deeply religious bunch, but also quite inquisitive. They were free to wonder "What if?"

And yet, while America's founders were deeply religious, they feared the tyranny of centralized power, even in religion. They had, not long before, come out of more than a thousand years of Roman Catholic oppression which had taught their flocks in a language most of them did not even understand. This was a church which murdered those who dared to attempt getting closer to God on their own. America's founders did not want a government based on this kind of subjugation, even if it were supposedly religious. This sentiment was a full century before Lord Acton made his most famous statement, and these Americans knew instinctively:

"POWER TENDS TO CORRUPT, AND ABSOLUTE POWER CORRUPTS ABSOLUTELY. GREAT MEN ARE ALMOST ALWAYS BAD MEN . . . ."

Along with the Renaissance (da Vinci, Galileo, and others), the Age of Enlightenment (John Locke, Thomas Hobbes, Jean-Jacques Rousseau, and others), the Protestant Reformation (Luther, Jan Hus, John Calvin, and others), the Americans were a scrappy bunch who had either grown up in this frontier land or had immigrated to it. The requirements of survival had made many of them into pragmatists— people with a hard, no-nonsense way of looking at the world which demanded practical results, rather than fanciful theories. This mix of worldviews and the variations which had occurred in a single lifetime cultivated a sense of change and destiny. Ideas like the dignity of the individual, equality of opportunity, limited government, the social contract, and the consent of the governed, had become fertile soil for the minds of those brave enough to consider other possibilities.

In 1761, James Otis, Jr. gave a 4–hour speech against the writs of assistance which gave British customs agents and military the ability to search anyone, any place, and at any time. His speech gave voice to what was to become the 4th Amendment protection against unreasonable searches and seizures. He argued that general, non-specific warrants were an assault on personal liberty. Years later, John Adams called Otis "a flame of fire!" In a very real sense, the American Revolution began with the words of James Otis, Jr.

"American Independence was then & there born."

*— JOHN ADAMS, WRITING OF THE 1761 SPEECH BY
JAMES OTIS, JR., AGAINST THE BRITISH WRITS OF
ASSISTANCE.*

The *Stamp Act* of 1765 imposed a tax on all papers and official documents in the American colonies but the tax did not apply in England. These and similar measures passed by English Parliament had created disagreeable burdens on the colonists. The *Declaratory Act* of 1766, coinciding with the repeal of the *Stamp Act*, reaffirmed the distant Parliament's belief that their taxing authority was the same in the American colonies as in England. This created a thorn in the minds of the Americans which produced more intellectual indignation than any other form of oppression. In fact, the language of the *Declaratory Act* was used repeatedly by America's Founding Fathers to express their displeasure at the arrogance of those in the homeland.

Parliament attempted to put the rowdy colonies back in their rightful place via the *Declaratory Act* by establishing for itself and the crown, the "full power and authority to make laws and statutes of sufficient force and validity to bind the colonies and people of America, subjects of the crown of Great Britain, in all cases whatsoever . . . ." This last clause—"in all cases whatsoever"—both frightened and angered some of the more astute Americans, while their fellows celebrated the apparent victory of the *Stamp Act's* repeal. Those more aware Americans knew that the implications of the wording provided them with a ticking time bomb of future tyranny.

The chief contention felt by the Americans was that government had become arbitrary, set by whim to create *ad hoc* rules to suit the selfish desires of those who govern.

One of the many reasons listed in the *Declaration of Independence*, ten years later, included a reference to the *Declara-*

tory Act: "For suspending our own legislatures, and declaring themselves invested with power to legislate for us in all cases whatsoever." The meaning of that clause implied that Parliament and the crown could do whatever they wanted and America had no recourse. Effectively, Parliament had declared America to be a slave state with which the imperial government could do as it pleased. Some of the Americans knew that this would eventually spell their doom. Divorce from England seemed the only realistic solution.

REMOTE AND ALOOF

England was weeks away by sailing ships—as disconnected as modern man is from the planets. The British government seemed cold and detached—entirely blind to the needs and concerns of the colonists. Because the Americans were so far away, the government seemed to itself free to deprive them of the liberties enjoyed by their local countrymen—those living on the English island. It was as if there were three standards of law: one for the nobility, one for the common man of England, and one for the lowly colonials.

The Americans had no say in Parliament—no representation. Yet, they were taxed in ways not suffered by their brothers in England. The uneven treatment provided even more reasons for discontent.

Besides the distance from England, the Americans had become squeezed in another manner, between sea and an artificial barrier established by the British government. The royal Proclamation of 1763, not long after the French and Indian War, prevented Americans from expanding past the Appalachian Mountains. That royal decree was ignored by many Americans, especially those who had already purchased lands or had received land grants.

It seemed that every possible freedom was being met with oppression.

In 1764, Parliament passed the *Sugar Act* (a new tax on molasses), and the *Currency Act* (a law which curtailed the colonial use of paper money). The second of these laws caused the greatest concern, because commerce in the American colonies was made increasingly difficult by all of the British rules concerning commerce—restricting with whom the colonies could trade and how trade could be conducted. The ability of the hardworking colonists to make an honest living was being stifled by all of these regulations. The Americans resorted to bartering, but even that method of exchange proved increasingly unsatisfactory. The preferred gold and silver coin had become rare in America and for England to demand these as payment in trade made commerce next to impossible.

The *Stamp Act* of 1765 added a tax to all paper goods sold, all contracts written, and all bills of lading with their accompanying shipments, and a stamp was affixed to the paper to show that the tax had been paid. Two days later, Parliament passed the *Quartering Act*, which required citizens of the American colonies to house British troops in their homes.

Because the *English Bill of Rights* (1689) had made it illegal to impose taxes on British citizens without the consent of Parliament, the American colonists felt that their lack of representation in Parliament made these new taxes illegal. The rallying cry, "no taxation without representation," became a common theme in colonial resistance. The common Englishman of the home island had representation in Parliament and thus suffered none of these burdens. But the requirement to house troops in their homes made the Americans feel abused on a far more personal level.

As an example of the abuses suffered, one article in an Edinburgh, Scotland newspaper reported that three ships were seized by the British military for reason that they carried official documents which did not have tax stamps affixed to them. The livelihood of the ships' owners, their officers and crew were destroyed by the lack of an official stamp on each document. The punishment seemed far out of proportion with the offense.

When the *Stamp Act* was repealed the following year, Parliament issued the *Declaratory Act* in order to reassert its own power over the colonies. But the English homeland had its own share of unrest. Because of a poor harvest, the "Bread and Butter" riots of September 1766 created chaos all across England, a result of the ongoing Little Ice Age (AD 1350–1850).

Because of the British government's debts from the Seven Years' War (including the French and Indian War), Parliament passed the *Townshend Acts* of 1767 to gain even more revenue from the colonies. And they sent more soldiers to help ensure payment was made. Even more Americans would be forced to invite British "Red Coats" into their homes, to eat their food and to disrupt their daily lives.

A scuffle between British troops and New Yorkers occurred on January 17, 1770, in what became known as the "Battle of Golden Hill." No one was killed, but several people were injured. Nearly seven weeks later—March 5—British troops in Boston fired upon an unruly and abusive mob, killing five civilians. This Boston Massacre inflamed the rhetoric within the colonies, creating far more riotous anger than reasoned action. Many of the citizens of Boston wanted the soldiers executed for their "massacre." So great were their passions that even Loyalist attorneys were afraid to defend the soldiers. Finally, John Adams took up the case and ably defended, first their Captain Preston, and then the soldiers as a group. Preston was found not guilty, while only two of the soldiers were found guilty of the reduced charge of manslaughter.

Adams had long been a staunch defender of the presumption of innocence until proven guilty. The fact that his personal sentiments sided with those promoting liberty, he believed very strongly in honor and evidence. "Facts are stubborn things;" said Adams, "and whatever may be our wishes, our inclinations, or the dictates of our passion, they cannot alter the state of facts and evidence." Furthermore, he said, "It is more important that innocence be protected than it is that guilt be punished, for guilt and crimes are so frequent in this world that they cannot all be punished. But if innocence itself is brought to the bar and condemned, perhaps to die, then the citizen will say, 'whether I do good or whether I do evil is immaterial, for innocence itself is no protection,' and if such an idea as that were to take hold in the mind of the citizen that would be the end of security whatsoever." John Adams would go on to become the second president of these United States.

The Revolutionary War which was about to start would last for nearly eight and a half years—almost an entire decade. That long war, against the most formidable military force in the world, would take its toll on all who lived in the American colonies. There were many critical events throughout the conflict, some of them including the Siege of Boston, the New Jersey Campaign, the Saratoga Campaign, Greene's Southern Campaign, and the Yorktown Campaign.

There have been many books on America's Revolution and the war which accompanied societal change. This book hopes to provide the reader with a fresh perspective on the men and women who risked their honor, their fortunes and their lives to help create a new nation, under God, conceived in liberty so that even the smallest minority—the individual

—would be protected from the whim of tyranny, even that found in a democracy.

Though they had an imperfect beginning, some of America's Founding Fathers saw a future time when all men would walk free, to pursue life, liberty and the happiness derived from the fruits of their own labor.

> *"But what do we mean by the American Revolution? Do we mean the American war? The Revolution was effected before the war commenced. The Revolution was in the minds and hearts of the people; a change in their religious sentiments of their duties and obligations. . . . This radical change in the principles, opinions, sentiments, and affections of the people, was the real American Revolution"*
>
> — *JOHN ADAMS, LETTER TO HEZEKIAH NILES,*
> *FEBRUARY 13, 1818.*

When Benjamin Franklin left Independence Hall in Philadelphia after the convention which gave America its current constitution, one woman asked him, "Well, Doctor, what have you given us—a Republic or a Monarchy?" Franklin replied, "A Republic, if you can keep it."

UPRISING

*I*n the 21st century, it is hard to imagine what life was like in the 18th century. The Old World of Europe had a rich and complicated heritage fraught with difficulties and corruption. But despite the many problems, humanity was making progress on several fronts—especially in science, religion, and government.

OUR 18TH CENTURY WORLD

Englishmen had enjoyed five centuries of relative freedom. Throughout that half a millennium, subjects of the British crown fought to increase the liberties they enjoyed, struggling against the inevitable corruption of power. Philosophers began to discuss the relationships between governments and the governed. Old assumptions were being questioned and new frontiers in thought were being pushed beyond previous limits.

Nowhere do we see such advancements more clearly than in the sciences, including the field of mathematics.

In the late 17th century, Newton (1643–1727) and

Leibniz (1646–1714) had discovered the concepts of calculus, forever changing the face of mathematics. The notations of Leibniz, which we use today, were still a relatively new idea in the colleges of the 18th century.

Englishman, John Flamsteed (1646–1719), developed one of the earliest, modern star catalogs from which a star atlas— the *Atlas Coelestis*—was published ten years after his death.

Even the Americans had contributed to the advancement of science, perhaps most famously with Benjamin Franklin (1706–1790) and his early experiments with electricity (1752).

Medicine was still a brutal art in the 18th century. Cleanliness and sterilization would not become important to doctors until the mid-19th century. Thus, in the 18th century patients frequently died from infections which could have been easily prevented today. Vaccines did not exist until Englishman, Edward Jenner (1749–1823), first discovered the technique in 1796.

As the American Revolution unfolded in the New World, Frenchman Antoine Lavoisier (1743–1794), in the Old World, was upending the paradigm of *phlogiston* (a theoretical element supposedly released during the burning of a substance), plus identifying and naming the elements oxygen and hydrogen. Lavoisier also helped to develop the metric system of measures.

Though the primary Age of Exploration had ended, British naval officer, James Cook (1728–1779), added greater understanding of the Pacific Ocean with his three voyages of discovery (1768–1771, 1772–1775, 1776–1779).

The struggle between despotic, arbitrary power and individual liberties was about to have its greatest single breakthrough. This advancement for humanity would take place in the British, New World colonies of America.

From the start of the 1700s to the start of the American

Revolutionary War in 1775, the population of the British colonies expanded by a factor of ten to roughly 2 million of European descent. The population in England was approaching 8 million at the time of the American war. This meant that British citizens in the 13 American colonies stood as a significant percentage of English free men, yet they did not have the same rights as their fellow countrymen. That inequality would end up destroying the link between England and her colonies.

AMERICA'S FOUNDING FATHERS AT THE START OF THE FRENCH AND INDIAN WAR

The year 1754 marked the beginning of a conflict that proved to be a turning point in the destiny of the American colonies — the French and Indian War, which became the true first World War known in Europe as the Seven Years' War. A bitter rivalry between the British and French empires had come to a head on the North American continent. The focal point for their conflict was the Ohio River valley. Three empires occupied North America — the Spanish in the South and West, the French in the center from Louisiana to Canada, and the British in the East. The following is a snapshot of America's founders at the start of this crucial war:

GEORGE WASHINGTON (1732–1799)

In 1754, Washington was a young, loyal, British officer, 22 years of age. He would become America's first president some 35 years later. In this year, however, Washington's actions under British command, as lieutenant colonel in the Virginia Regiment, led to the French and Indian War (an American conflict) and ultimately to the larger Seven Years' War (a global conflict).

Washington gained an early victory and was named commander of the regiment on the death of his superior officer, but later was captured. Though he resigned his commission, he volunteered as an aide to General Edward Braddock.

BENJAMIN FRANKLIN (1706–1790)

Franklin was 48 and enjoying a bit of celebrity in Europe and the Americas for his work on electricity two years earlier. Franklin was also becoming more political as he led the delegation from Pennsylvania to the Albany Congress — a convention which sought to improve colonial relations with native tribes and to establish coordinated defenses against the belligerent French.

THOMAS JEFFERSON (1743–1826)

Jefferson was a young boy of 11, living as a British citizen on the family's estate at the Shadwell Plantation in the Virginia colony. He would go on to become America's third president in another 47 years.

JOHN ADAMS (1735–1826)

Adams was a teenager, age 19. Three years earlier, he had started his university education at Harvard College, learning to read the works of Plato, Thucydides, Tacitus, and Cicero in the Greek and Latin of their times. It was not until some years later that he decided on a career as a lawyer. But in 1754, he felt some guilt at not being a part of the Massachusetts Militia to help in the French and Indian War, later writing, "I longed more ardently to be a Soldier than I ever did to be a Lawyer."

He was not only America's second president, some 43 years later, he was also the father of the sixth president, John Quincy Adams (1767–1848).

JAMES MADISON (1751–1836)

Madison was yet an infant, age 3.

Madison was the eldest of what would later become twelve siblings, though many of them would not survive to adulthood. Several years later, the family would build a new home called Montpelier, on their Belle Grove Plantation in Virginia colony, near Port Conway. As a rich plantation owner's son, he was destined to have private tutoring for his early education.

He would go on to become America's fourth president, 55 years later.

JOHN JAY (1745–1829)

At age 9, Jay was living in New Rochelle, New York, studying under Pierre Stoupe, an Anglican priest. His mother had home schooled him until age 8, in their home in Rye, New York.

He would go on to become America's first Supreme Court chief justice, 35 years later.

ALEXANDER HAMILTON (1755–1804)

In 1754, Hamilton's mother was thought to have been pregnant with the future first Secretary of the Treasury. There is some uncertainty regarding his year of birth. Some sources cite a birth date of January 11, 1755, while others quote 1757. Born out of wedlock, Hamilton was orphaned at age 13.

Hamilton's mother, Rachel Faucett Lavien (c.1727–1768), had been married to a far older man, John Lavien, but she later had two sons with a failed merchant named John Hamilton, even though she was not married to him. Alexander was the second of those two sons.

THE FRENCH AND INDIAN WAR AND THE SEVEN YEARS' WAR

The North American French and Indian War (1754–1763) became the flashpoint which led to the expanded conflict known later as the Seven Years' War (1756–1763). In the mid-18th century, three nations vied for global supremacy — Spain, France, and Great Britain. Though Spain's influence had been waning for over a century, it remained a major global power with colonies around the world. In North America, France and England were the primary powers and each wanted to establish their own dominance there as well as in the world-at-large.

The focal point for the French and Indian War was the Ohio River Valley, the frontier between the British colonies and New France, present day Canada. Both powers claimed the territory as their own. The French considered the valley crucial to connect their holdings in New France and territories in Louisiana and built military forts to counter the British efforts to expand westward. In 1753, the French advanced south and west from Fort Niagara on Lake Ontario, driving out English traders and claiming the Ohio River Valley for France. That same year, Virginia Governor Robert Dinwiddie learned the French built Fort Presque Isle near Lake Erie and Fort Le Boeuf on territory claimed by Virginia. The Governor sent an eight-man expedition under Lt. Colonel George Washington to warn the French to withdraw. The French refused and instead built Fort Duquesne near present-day Pittsburgh at the confluence of the Allegheny and Monongahela Rivers—the two main tributaries of the Ohio River. Washington returned to the Ohio Valley in 1754 with 160 men and ambushed the French, killing their commanding officer and many men. Roughly a month later, Washington's forces were similarly overwhelmed by hundreds of French and Native Americans at Fort Necessity. As Washington was forced to capitulate, he had no idea that this skirmish would set the world on fire and lead most of the British colonies in America to break with England a little over a decade after the conclusion of this conflict.

BELLIGERENTS ALIGNED WITH GREAT BRITAIN

- British America
  - British West Indies
  - Brunswick-Wolfenbüttel
  - Carnatic Sultanate
  - East India Company
  - Filipino rebels
  - Great Britain
  - Hanover
  - Hesse-Kassel
  - Iroquois Confederacy
  - Nizam of Hyderabad
  - Portugal
  - Portuguese India
  - Prussia
  - Russia (from 1762)
  - Schaumburg-Lippe
  - Viceroyalty of Brazil

BELLIGERENTS ALIGNED WITH FRANCE

•Abenaki tribe
  •Algonquin nation
  •Austria
  •Bengal Subah
  •Colony of Canada
  •Dutch East India Company
  •France
  •French East India Company
  •French West Indies
  •Hesse-Darmstadt
  •Kalmykia
  •Mi'kmaq tribe
  •Mughal Empire
  •Naples
  •New France
  •New Spain
  •Odawa tribe
  •Ojibwe tribes
  •Russia (until 1762)
  •Savoy-Sardinia
  •Saxony
  •Shawnee tribes
  •Spain
  •Sweden
  •Viceroyalty of Peru
  •Wabanaki Confederacy

Washington's capitulation at Fort Necessity predicted years of struggle for the British and colonial forces. The colonies were not prepared to wage war against the French and their allies and supplying British forces with food and arms was expensive and difficult. In 1755, the French defeated Major General Edward Braddock at the Monongahela River in the Ohio River Valley. By the next year, the conflict spread worldwide to the Caribbean, northern Europe, the Mediterranean, and India.

Britain nearly doubled its national debt by the end of the war in 1763. Through 1757 and 1758, Britain poured money and resourced into the conflict, sending thousands of British regulars to the American colonies. The tide turned for the British, who were victorious in a string of battles at Louisbourg, Ticonderoga, Pittsburgh, Fort Niagara, and Fort Frontenac under the military leadership of William Pitt the Elder. By 1759, the British laid siege to Quebec, taking control of present-day Canada.

In 1762, Spain entered the war allied with France but Spain failed to reverse British gains. Indeed, British expeditions went on to defeat these allied forces around the world in India, the French Antilles, Spanish Cuba in the Caribbean, and Spanish Manila in the Philippines. In February 1763, Britain, France, and Spain signed the Treaty of Paris, ending the war and ceding French territory in North America to Britain including territories east of the Mississippi inhabited by Native Americans while Spain ceded its territory in present-day Florida. This enormous turnover in territorial control solidified England as a world power, but also led to a number of problems that culminated in the American Revolution.

This global conflict was, in a very real sense, a world war. Even Winston Churchill, in the 20th century, referred to the Seven Years' War as the "first world war." Because of the complexity and scope of these hostilities, the cost to Great Britain was extreme. British Parliament was desperate to recoup the funds used to pay for this carnage.

PROCLAMATION OF 1763

In an attempt to appease Native American tribes which had been aligned with the French during the war, King George III issued a royal decree setting out how the territories acquired by the Treaty of Paris would be governed. The proclamation set the Appalachian Mountains as the boundary for the Thirteen Colonies, declaring the area to the west as "Indian Reserve." Only the British Crown could purchase or grant land west of this line and colonists were forbidden from settling there.

George Washington was among those who were angry regarding the *Proclamation of 1763*. He and many of his fellow Virginians had been promised lands for their services to Great Britain and to the Virginia colony. British land specu-lators objected as well and, joining with their colonial brethren, lobbied the crown to adjust the border westward. In a series of treaties with Native Americans, the border was adjusted. Even so, Americans were understandably angry at the imposition of this seemingly arbitrary ruling which created a betrayal of promises made.

Many colonists simply ignored the royal edict. Either they had already purchased land in the forbidden region, had started to build, had received land grants, or merely did not want to be restricted in their desire for new lands and new opportunities.

SUGAR ACT OF 1764

The Seven Years' War had been painfully expensive for Great Britain. One year after the war, British Parliament exacted a tax on molasses in the American colonies. The Molasses Act of 1733 had proven ineffective, so the British government cut the tax in half and spent more on enforcement and collection. American colonists resented the tax, especially during a time of economic depression. The American colonies also suffered from the local portion of the Seven Years' War — the French and Indian War. This burden on top of the squeeze the British crown had placed on American desires to expand westward, had created a simmering anger toward the selfishness of the British government. Certainly, the colonists were looking out for themselves, but the lack of representation in Parliament made the economic injury even more painful. At least Englishmen on the home island could have a say in their own taxation.

CURRENCY ACT OF 1764

The Currency Act of 1764 imposed restrictions on printing fiat money as a result of British merchants' complaints about having to accept devalued American currency. Printing more currency than is backed by the goods in circulation creates a condition called "inflation" which lowers the value of each unit of currency. The *Currency Act of 1764* was an extension of a previous law of 1751. The colonists had used paper money ("bills of credit") to pay for the expenses incurred from the French and Indian War and to pay for goods imported from Great Britain. The effect of this law was to tighten the economy of the American colonies so that it became more difficult to conduct business.

Colonial agents in London, including Benjamin Franklin, sought to repeal or amend the *Currency Act*. The New York colony, for instance, later complained that the *Quartering Act of 1765* had become impossible under the current economic conditions. Thus, in 1770, Parliament amended the law to allow the colony to issue currency for public debts only. Similar amendments relaxed the economic restraints so that, by the start of war, the *Currency Act* was more of an emotional burden than an economic one.

STAMP ACT OF 1765

This Act required that many printed materials and paper products include an official stamp to be paid with British currency instead of colonial paper money. Such paper products included all legal documents, newspapers, magazines, and even playing cards. This was yet another method the British government used to raise revenue to pay for the costly Seven Years' War, including its American segment, the French and Indian War. This made conducting business in the colonies even more difficult. Of all the uncomfortable laws passed up to this point, the *Stamp Act* generated the most universally negative response. So great was the dislike for this law amongst the colonists that they held a congress in New York in order to draft a petition to Parliament and the king. The cost of official stamps was great enough for many colonial merchants to risk conducting business without them. A few examples of heavy-handed enforcement did more to enrage the colonists than to promote compliance. A sufficient number of colonial Americans boycotted or threatened to boycott British goods that English merchants also pressured Parliament, which repealed the law.

"If you comply with the Act by using Stamped Papers, you fix, you rivet perpetual Chains upon your unhappy Country. You unnecessarily, voluntarily establish the detestable Precedent, which those who have forged your Fetters ardently wish for, to varnish the future Exercise of this new claimed Authority . . . . If you quietly bend your Necks to that Yoke, you prove your-

selves ready to receive any Bondage to which your Lords and Masters shall please to subject you."

> — *JOHN DICKINSON (A FARMER IN PENNSYLVANIA), 1765, WRITING AGAINST THE STAMP ACT.*

DECLARATORY ACT OF 1766

With the repeal of the unpopular *Stamp Act*, Parliament attempted to reassert its authority over the colonies. The Act was a simple declaration of supremacy of the British government over the people of the colonies because Parliament saw the revolt against the *Stamp Act* as an affront to their authority. While many in the colonies celebrated the repeal of the *Stamp Act*, many others were concerned by the tone and content of the *Declaratory Act* which accompanied that repeal.

The preamble provides: "An act for the better securing the dependency of his majesty's dominions in America upon the crown and parliament of Great Britain." The British government made clear its intent to force the colonies into utter dependency. But the line which most concerned the colonists continued, "[Parliament had] full power and authority to make laws and statutes of sufficient force and validity to bind the colonies and people of America, subjects of the crown of Great Britain, in all cases whatsoever" making the colonists in America powerless to the arbitrary whims of the British government.

TOWNSHEND ACTS OF 1767–68

The Townshend Acts were a series of laws for increasing revenue and punishing New York for non-compliance with the *Quartering Act of 1765*. This set of 5 laws was named after Charles Townshend (1725–1767), the Chancellor of the Exchequer. Great Britain needed more revenue and those in Parliament despised the unruly colonists for resisting the will of the government. The list of laws included in this group may vary depending on the scholar discussing them, but the following 5 are frequently cited as being included:

•*New York Restraining Act* (June 5, 1767) — Punishment for the New York colony's noncompliance of the *Quartering Act of 1765*. This law prevented New York from passing any new legislation until they had complied. New York felt the soldiers were no longer needed since the French and Indian War had already ended.

•*Revenue Act* (June 26, 1767) — New taxes on paper, lead, glass, painters' colors, and tea. This law also gave broad powers of enforcement by allowing at-will search and seizure of property thought to be contraband.

•*Indemnity Act* (June 29, 1767) — A method of protecting the collapse of the East India Company and of forcing the colonies to buy from that beleaguered company.

•*Commissioners of Customs Act* (June 29, 1767) — Establishment of a customs enforcement office in Boston to cut down on smuggling and to help enforce the collection of taxes.

•*Vice Admiralty Court Act* (July 6, 1768) — Created to aid in the prosecution of smugglers bypassing local courts. If the accused could not afford to travel to the court, or merely did not appear, he was considered automatically guilty. Sometimes not included with the first four in the collection called the *"Townshend Acts,"* especially because it was not enacted by Parliament and was passed with approval of the king several months after the death of Charles Townshend.

"Let these truths be indelibly impressed on your minds—that we cannot be HAPPY, without being FREE—that we cannot be free, without being secure in our property—*that we cannot be secure in our property,* if, without our consent, others may, as by right, take it away . . . . *Let us take care of our rights, and we therein take care of* our prosperity. *'SLAVERY IS EVER PRECEDED BY SLEEP.'"*

— *JOHN DICKINSON, 1767, RESPONSE TO TOWNSHEND ACTS.*

Dickinson's words reflected the deeply felt sentiments of the Americans and the philosophy behind the words used by America's Founding Fathers. Though this Pennsylvania farmer did not sign the *Declaration of Independence*, he was one of the leading minds behind the revolutionary spirit which became these United States of America.

"To divide and thus to destroy is the first political maxim in attacking those who are powerful by their union."

— *JOHN DICKINSON, LETTER #1 FROM A FARMER, 1767.*

"Some persons may think this act of no consequence, because the duties are so small. A fatal error. That is the very circumstance most alarming to me. For I am convinced, that the authors of this law would never have obtained an act to raise so trifling a sum as it must do, had they not intended by it to establish a precedent for future use. To console ourselves with the smallness of the duties, is to walk deliberately into the snare that is set for us, praising the neatness of the workmanship."

— *JOHN DICKINSON, LETTER #7, FROM A FARMER, 1767–1768.*

15

> *"The money said to be taken from us for our defense, may be employed to our injury."*
>
> — *JOHN DICKINSON, LETTER #9 FROM A FARMER,*
> 1767–1768.

BOSTON MASSACRE (1770)

On March 5, 1770, a British sentry had an argument with a colonist who insulted a British officer. When British reinforcements arrived, a menacing crowd of angry colonists surrounded the reinforcements and pelted them with rocks, ice, and whatever they could pick up from the scene. A British officer was struck, slipped on the ice, and fired his weapon. Shots rang out. Five civilians died and six more were wounded. The conflict and deaths can be seen in part as a result of the *Commissioners of Customs Act* passed by Parliament nearly three years earlier for the establishment of a customs enforcement office in Boston. The troops stationed there were responsible for helping the commissioners enforce the law. Future president John Adams defended the soldiers who were tried for murder. All but two soldiers were acquitted in trial. The two were convicted of the reduced charge of manslaughter. Though the incident involved only 5 fatalities, colonial resentment for the presence of troops made those deaths reason for even greater resentment.

TEA ACT (1773)

On April 27, 1773, Parliament passed a law to give the failing East India Company a monopoly on North American tea sales. The British East India Company provided the government with a relatively steady flow of revenues because all tea was forced to go through London to be taxed before he could be sold to the colonies. But the colonies bought an estimated 86% of their tea from the Dutch. Thus, this law made it possible for the British East India Company to sell directly to the Americans, but with the additional British taxes still in place.

Dutch imports were illegal, but they made up a thriving business which was threatened by the direct import of British tea. Others objected to the Townshend *Revenue Act* which taxed the British tea being imported. Both groups combined forces to oppose the import of tea from the British East India Company.

THE BOSTON TEA PARTY (1773)

On December 16, 1773, American rebels, angry about the *Revenue Act* tax on tea (one of the *Townshend Acts*), dumped an entire shipment of tea into Boston Harbor. Some rebels dressed as Mohawk warriors, a statement of identity as native Americans rather than as British subjects.

Though the tax was not significant, some colonists resented any taxation without being able to have a voice in Parliament. All factions of the British government were galvanized against the Americans for such a violent affront to their authority. They responded with what became known as the *Intolerable Acts*.

"Make yourselves sheep, and the wolves will eat you."

— *BENJAMIN FRANKLIN, NOVEMBER 1773.*

INTOLERABLE ACTS (1774)

In response to the Boston Massacre, Parliament passed five pieces of legislation included in the collection known as the "Intolerable Acts" (also sometimes known as the "Coercive Acts"):

•*The Boston Port Act* (March 30, 1774) — Forcefully closed Boston harbor until the destroyed tea had been paid for. Bostonians resented that all were being punished for the acts of a few.

•*Massachusetts Government Act* (May 20, 1774) — Revoked the Massachusetts charter and severely restricted the number of meetings which could be held. Government positions were to be held only by those appointed by the colonial governor, by Parliament, or by the king.

•*Administration of Justice Act* (May 20, 1774) — If any royal appointee were accused of a crime, the royal governor could order that their trial be held in a different venue (Great Britain, or some other location within the empire). Though any witnesses could be reimbursed for their travel expenses to and from the trial, they would not be paid for lost wages. George Washington infamously referred to this law as the "Murder Act" because it would allow such government agents to escape justice. Many colonists felt the law was entirely unnecessary after the fair trial of those accused of the Boston Massacre.

•*Quartering Act* (June 2, 1774) — Expanded on the previous *Quartering Act* (1765), giving governors even greater authority to select buildings for use by soldiers.

•*Quebec Act* (June 22, 1774) — Expanded the territory of the Province of Quebec to include a great deal of what is now the upper Midwest of these United States, overwriting the claims of American colonists on the Ohio River Valley. The former French citizens of the Canadian province were given greater liberties than those enjoyed by the British colonists who had fought against them during the French and Indian War.

> *"Liberty is essential to the happiness of a society, and therefore is our right."*

> — *JOHN DICKINSON*, LETTERS TO THE
> INHABITANTS OF THE BRITISH COLONIES, *JUNE*
> 1774.

> *"All artful rulers, who strive to extend their power beyond its just limits, endeavor to give to their attempts as much semblance of legality as possible."*

> — *JOHN DICKINSON.*

> *"The love of liberty is so natural to the human heart, that unfeeling tyrants think themselves obliged to accommodate their schemes as much as they can to the appearance of justice and reason, and to deceive those whom they resolve to destroy, or oppress, by presenting to them a miserable picture of freedom, then the inestimable original is lost."*

> — *JOHN DICKINSON.*

THE FIRST CONTINENTAL CONGRESS (1774)

In response to the *Intolerable Acts* (*Coercive Acts*) earlier in the year, twelve of the thirteen colonies met between September 5 and October 26, 1774. All of the colonies except Georgia were represented. Loyalists in Georgia wanted to avoid any involvement.

Two key factions argued on how to respond. One side wanted to repair the rift which had been developing between Great Britain and its colonies. The other side wanted to assert the rights of the colonists. Both sides found agreement in the need to end Parliament's abuses and to keep the rights established by the various colonial charters and by the English constitution which protected their fellow British subjects on the British Isles.

The colonies resolved to boycott all British goods starting December 1, 1774, unless the *Intolerable Acts* were repealed. If those laws were not repealed by September 10, 1775, then the colonies would stop exporting goods to Great Britain.

In anticipation of the need for a second continental congress, invitations were sent to Georgia, West Florida, East Florida, Nova Scotia, Quebec, and Saint John's Island. Of these, only Georgia would end up accepting the invitation.

TEST YOUR UNDERSTANDING

Answers to the following questions may be found in the Appendix.

1. How did the citizens of Massachusetts respond to the law passed in Parliament April 27, 1773, which gave the British East India Company a monopoly?
- Battle of Bunker Hill
- Invited visiting British officers to afternoon tea
- Boston Tea Party
- Petitioned the king to reconsider

2. Military leader, George Washington's actions in 1754 led to which difficulty?
- The French Revolution's Reign of Terror
- British conquest of India
- World War I
- The French and Indian War

3. Which act reasserted Parliament's supremacy over the colonies and included divisive wording which the Americans used in their *Declaration of Independence*?
- *Stamp Act* of 1765

•*Declaratory Act* of 1766
•*Revenue Act* of 1767
•*Tea Act* of 1773

4. Which law sought to force American colonists give British troops shelter?

•*Declaratory Act* (1766)
•*Massachusetts Government Act* (1774)
•*Quartering Act* (1765 and 1774)
•*Indemnity Act* (1767)

5. How many civilians were killed by British soldiers during the Boston Massacre?

•5
•17
•58
•319

SUMMING IT UP

In 1754, the British colonies in America were thrust into a war with the French and with many of the indigenous American tribes. That bloody fight escalated into a global conflict, later known as the Seven Years' War. When that war ended in 1763, Great Britain had incurred a massive debt and sought to reduce that debt through a series of taxes. Promises of land made to many of the colonists were broken by royal edict, the *Proclamation of 1763*.

The *Sugar Act*, *Currency Act*, and *Stamp Act* all made commerce more difficult for the colonists. Enforcement of the *Stamp Act* was particularly harsh with those possessing documents without the official stamp risking loss of property. Colonial representatives pleaded with Parliament to repeal the *Stamp Act* while many colonial merchants threatened to boycott British goods.

Though the *Stamp Act* was repealed the following year

(1766), the *Declaratory Act* set the tone for increasing escalation of British abuse of its colonies. The *Townshend Acts* of 1767 added even more burdens for the colonists through taxation and enforcement measures.

Late winter, 1770, saw the first flashpoint between the colonies and the growing presence of "red coats" (British soldiers) with the Boston Massacre. The *Tea Act of 1773* resulted in colonists in Massachusetts destroying an entire shipment of tea by dumping the cargo into Boston harbor.

In the months which followed, the British government added new laws called the *Intolerable Acts* which sought to punish Massachusetts, specifically, and all of the colonies, in general, for their disobedience. Late in 1774, 12 of the 13 British colonies, which later became these United States, sent representatives to the First Continental Congress to attempt to reconcile the differences between America and Great Britain.

Though no one at that congress wanted to break with the mother country, some colonists did not trust the British government to reduce tensions. They knew that a tyrant with power could not be coaxed to be lenient once its emotions had been stirred.

WAR IS DECLARED

*C*itizens of the Massachusetts colony decided to bypass the official government in Boston and establish their own Massachusetts Provincial Congress in Concord. In anticipation of a negative British response, colonial authorities ordered local militias to train just in case the British army escalated hostilities.

On February 9, 1775, British Parliament declared that the Massachusetts colony was in a state of rebellion. However, not everyone in England agreed with the harsh treatment of the Americans. On March 22, 1775, Irish-British member of Parliament, Edmund Burke, spoke to the legislative body on behalf of the colonies seeking reconciliation. He was unable, however, to sway his fellow ministers to reduce the growing tensions between the government and the colonies across the ocean.

Because of the February declaration by Parliament and the growing insurrection, the British military sought to reduce the risk of armed resistance by capturing the colonial stockpile of munitions.

British troop movements on April 7, 1775 alerted the

colonial Patriots that a potential crackdown may then have been in motion. Patriots in Concord began moving their munitions to another location.

On April 14, 1775, General Thomas Gage received orders from England to disarm the Massachusetts rebels and to arrest Samuel Adams, John Hancock, and the other insurrection leaders.

PAUL REVERE'S RIDE

In the weeks leading up to the first conflict of the American Revolutionary War, silversmith and colonial industrialist Paul Revere (1735–1818), arranged with the North Church Sexton, Robert Newman (1752–1804), to set out a signal once British troop movements were underway. Revere was one of the Sons of Liberty, the activist group responsible for many of the actions taken against British oppression, including the Boston Tea Party.

Late, on the evening of April 18, 1775, Revere received word that the British troops were preparing to move, so he crossed the Charles River under cover of darkness to begin his assigned mission. At the time, it had been made illegal to cross the river at night. Like so many American Patriots, he felt justified in breaking any minor laws in order to follow the supreme laws governing the British empire. Paul Revere and fellow Patriot, William Dawes (1745–1799), set out to warn as many people as possible that the British regulars were coming. By the end of the night, more than three dozen riders had been set in motion to warn the citizens of every nearby township.

About midnight, Revere arrived in Lexington, some 9.3 miles (15 kilometers) west of Boston's Old North Church. He was there to meet with Samuel Adams and John Hancock. The number of British troops in motion seemed far too many to be merely arresting the two leaders. The men suspected that the rebel capital, Concord, must be their target. From there, Revere and Dawes assisted in triggering an alarm system by which much of eastern Massachusetts became aware of the approaching British troops.

Though Revere, Dawes, and one other were captured on their way to Concord, all three were eventually able to escape.

LEXINGTON & CONCORD

Just after sunrise, April 19, 1775, 700 British regulars under the command of Lt. Colonel Francis Smith engaged a small band of militia on Lexington Commons. Eight of the Patriots were killed, while only one of the British troops died. The militia fell back allowing the British troops to proceed on to Concord, the North Bridge of which was another 5.5 miles (9 kilometers) farther west.

As the British troops neared Concord, they split into several companies in order to search for the munitions said to be stored there. Around 11 o'clock, at the North Bridge across the Concord River, a hundred soldiers of three British companies met 400 Patriot militiamen. Though there were casualties on both sides, the British were sufficiently outnumbered to retreat back the main force in Concord.

After having searched Concord thoroughly and unable to find the munitions, the British forces attempted to return to Boston. However, arriving Patriots from other towns continued to fire upon the British troops making their retreat even more perilous.

Upon arriving at Lexington, Smith's 700 were joined by another 1,000 British regulars under Brigadier General Hugh Percy. Together, they continued on to Boston, being harried the entire way back. Once they had arrived at Boston, the

Patriots began to blockade the narrow land bridge to Boston proper. And then the Patriots laid siege to the city.

BOSTON & BUNKER HILL

The oldest part of Boston, known as Charles Town, sat on a peninsula at the mouths of the Charles and Mystic Rivers at the edge of Boston Harbor. On that peninsula were two hills known today as Bunker Hill and Breed's Hill. After the initial battles near Lexington and Concord, local British forces were confined to Boston.

Nearly two months after the battles of Lexington and Concord, colonial forces, which had continued their siege of Boston, learned on June 13, 1775, that the British were planning to capture some hills overlooking the harbor in order to give them a strategic advantage.

Using stealth, Patriot forces moved onto the peninsula, occupying Breed's Hill and setting up protective barriers across the peninsula to prevent the British from escaping by land.

On the morning of June 17, 1775, British officers became fully aware of the colonial forces arrayed across the Charlestown peninsula.

American commander William Prescott famously told his fellow Americans, "Do not fire until you see the whites of their eyes." The first two waves of attacks were stopped by the colonial forces, killing a great many of the British troops. The third attack succeeded only because the colonial forces had run out of ammunition. Patriots retreated past Bunker Hill, yielding full control over the peninsula back to the British forces.

Though the British were victorious, it was a bittersweet win—one which made them far more cautious in future battles. The supposedly ill-trained colonial militia was a far more effective opponent than they had thought possible. The aftermath was a stalemate in the midst of a long siege to liberate Boston from the British. Americans: 115 killed, 305 wounded. British: 19 officers killed, 62 officers wounded; 207 soldiers killed, 766 soldiers wounded.

LOYALISTS

Scholars estimate that the population of the 13 American colonies in 1776 was about 2.5 million with about 19% African-American (~475,000), roughly 92% of which were slaves (~437,000). More modern estimates, most notably by historian Robert Calhoon, place the number of Loyalists as high as 20% of the white population (~405,000). An estimated 500,000 additional people were pacifists who preferred not to get involved in the conflict. By comparison, the maximum number of Patriot militia was about 40,000; on their shoulders rested the fate of the nation.

If these numbers are accurate, then the number of Patriots standing behind those soldiers was as high as 1.1 million Americans.

Why would there be so many in America who remained loyal to the tyrannical government of King George III? Loyalty to one's country is a powerful emotion. And this emotion can contribute to a "normalcy bias" — the tendency to minimize or disbelieve warnings of imminent threats. Many German citizens fell into this category in the late 1930s as their popular, national socialist government began to reveal its own tyranny. It is only natural for people to continue to give support despite mounting evidence against that support.

American humorist, Mark Twain (1835–1910), has been misquoted as saying, "It's easier to fool people than to convince them that they have been fooled." What he actually said, in his autobiography, means much the same thing: "How easy it is to make people believe a lie, and how hard it is to undo that work again!"

Certainty has a nasty habit of preventing people from seeing the evidence which would otherwise prove them to be wrong. Some Loyalists may have felt that King George III and Parliament were justified in cracking down on the "lawless" American rebels. With such certainty, they may not have made the connection to the facts that English Common Law prohibited the government from taxing its citizens without the approval of Parliament, but that the legislative body was supposed to represent all of the people — not merely those who lived in England. And by the 1770s, the American colonies were a significant percentage of the entire population of the British Empire.

The opposite of the Loyalists' normalcy bias is the attitude of alarmism — those who expect the worst possible scenario. Certainly, there were a few who fit into this category — perhaps Samuel Adams and the Sons of Liberty. Their reactions to the increasing tyranny may well have brought about even more tyranny from a reactionary Parliament. Thus, egoistic certainty on both sides seems to have contributed to the escalation of hostilities.

Some Loyalists proclaimed their devotion to the crown, letting British military officers know that they were quite willing to assist in defending the lawful British government against the American upstarts. However, the British military remained wary of possible double agents and were not anxious to make ready use of American support.

Even so, as many as 25,000 American Loyalists joined the British army in order to fight the rebels.

THE SECOND CONTINENTAL CONGRESS

Because the British government had placed a limit of one public meeting a year, the First Continental Congress, held in late 1774, scheduled in advance the Second Continental Congress to be held the following year. Peyton Randolph was elected as the first president of the Congress. There were as many as 60 attendees, including Benjamin Franklin, John Hancock, and Thomas Jefferson.

This second annual meeting started May 10, 1775 — roughly three weeks after the battles of Lexington and Concord, and a little over a month before the Battle of Bunker Hill.

Despite the original intention of holding a congress of only several weeks' duration, the Second Continental Congress ended up becoming the *de facto* national government for nearly 6 years, throughout the Revolutionary War, until March 1, 1781. British hostilities had made this inevitable because the British government had made it clear that it cared not to negotiate, but to enforce their will with force.

And it was this Second Continental Congress which took responsibility for establishing an army; for composing documents of intent and treaties; and for giving birth to a new nation called these "United Colonies" — a name they would use for the first year of this new nation's existence. In fact, currency printed from the start of the Second Continental Congress until February 1777 carried this name. It was not until the *Declaration of Independence* in July 1776 that the name of these "United States" would become emblazoned on official documents for all the world to see.

On June 14, 1775, the Second Continental Congress instituted the Continental Army to protect the interests of the British colonies so long as Parliament seemed unsympathetic to the rights of Englishmen living overseas.

Three weeks later, on July 5, 1775, the *Olive Branch Petition* was approved by this Congress. Though a few colonists had been ready to break with Great Britain, most delegates wanted to give the mother country another opportunity to help repair the rift which had formed between government and the governed.

The following day, July 6, saw the completion of their statement to the British government — a document called, *Declaration of the Causes and Necessity of Taking Up Arms*. Various drafts and text had been written by John Rutledge, Thomas Jefferson, and John Dickinson. This document explained the reasons for the conflict and vowed that arms would be laid down "when hostilities shall cease on the part of the Aggressors." The Americans felt that they were being thorough, methodical, and reasonable.

> *"Our attachment to no Nation upon earth should supplant our attachment to liberty."*
>
> — JOHN DICKINSON WITH THOMAS JEFFERSON,
> DECLARATION OF THE CAUSES AND NECESSITY
> OF TAKING UP ARMS, JULY 6, 1775.

Two days later, on July 8, the *Olive Branch Petition* was signed by the congressional delegates, and both documents were sent to England.

Up until July 1775, only 12 of the original 13 contiguous colonies were in attendance. After July, Georgia finally sent its own delegation to the Second Continental Congress to join in a boycott of trade with Britain.

The following month, on August 23, 1775, upon hearing of the Battle of Bunker Hill, King George III declared that a state of rebellion existed in parts of the continental colonies. When the *Olive Branch Petition* was finally received by the British government, the king refused to read it, but instead declared the colonists to be traitors.

FORMING THE MILITIA AND CONTINENTAL ARMY

After the Second Continental Congress had been in attendance for a little over a month, they established the Continental Army on June 14, 1775. This was only three days before the Battle of Bunker Hill, during the Siege of Boston. Because the Americans had only yet decided to protect their interests within the British Empire, this army was merely a force to carry out that protection.

But when a people protect themselves from an oppressive government, it should not seem surprising when that tyrannical government objects. Monarchs fully expect compliance from their subjects; those who objected were to be put down because any insubordination could not be tolerated by a government, even if that government did not fully follow its own laws.

The well respected Boston attorney, John Adams, could have nominated his cousin, Samuel Adams, or Sam's associate, John Hancock, as commander of the Continental Army, but he chose, instead, George Washington.

Congress agreed with the Bostonian's recommendation and selected Washington as their Commander-in-Chief because of his experience in battle and because he seemed to be far more level-headed than John Hancock of Massachusetts. Hancock was one of the leaders of the rebel government in the Massachusetts colony who had helped to stir up colonial animosity against British officials. Washington was seen as a more moderate leader who could help to unite all of the colonies in their common purpose.

When General Washington joined the Patriot forces laying siege to Boston, he let those who desired to enlist know that they "are now Troops of the United Provinces of North America," and he made it clear his desire "that all Distinctions of Colonies will be laid aside; so that one and the same Spirit may animate the whole, and the only Contest be, who shall render, on this great and trying occasion, the most essential service to the Great and common cause in which we are all engaged." These were written in his General Orders of July 4, 1775 — precisely one year before the signing of the *Declaration of Independence.*

Each colony had its own militia to protect its borders and its interests. From the very start, each state considered itself to be at least a semi-sovereign province within the broader British Empire. When the Continental Army was first established, it included soldiers and officers from the 12 colonies, and later also from Georgia when it joined the other colonies against Great Britain.

TEST YOUR UNDERSTANDING

Answers to the following questions may be found in the Appendix.

1. What was the original name used by the Second Continental Congress for their new nation?
   •Do Not Tread on Me
   •The 13 Colonies
   •E Pluribus Unum
   •United Colonies

2. Which colony was the last to join the effort against Great Britain's tyranny?
   •Virginia
   •Massachusetts
   •Georgia

•New York

3. Why was George Washington chosen to lead the Continental Army?

•Because of his military experience and his ability to bring people together.

•Because he was friends with fellow Virginian, Thomas Jefferson.

•Because he had started the whole mess with the French and Indian War.

•Because he was the first president of these United States.

4. What was one chief reason for the British to send troops to Concord, Massachusetts?

•To arrest John Adams and Thomas Jefferson.

•To show the rowdy colonials who was in charge.

•To capture and destroy the munitions held there.

•To provoke the colonial rebels into a fight.

5. Why were local militias in Massachusetts ordered to train in early 1775?

•Practice makes perfect.

•To provoke the British military into taking the next step.

•To let the British know that they were ready for anything.

•Just in case the British army increased their aggression.

SUMMING IT UP

Colonial forces in Massachusetts prepared for the worst by having their militias train and by stockpiling munitions. British troop movements in spring of 1775 raised suspicions of an attack on the unofficial colonial government. Though General Gage had been ordered to arrest the rebel leaders, his chief objective was to disarm the unruly citizens. Forewarned, colonial leaders had the munitions moved from Concord.

Colonial Patriots Paul Revere and William Dawes alerted militias west of Boston when the British troops were on the move. The first shots were fired near Lexington, killing nine, mostly colonial militia. Another battle occurred at Concord's North Bridge.

British withdrawal all the way back to Boson was met with a series of colonial attacks culminating in the Siege of Boston, blocking the land route away from the city. In a stealth raid, colonial forces penetrated into the peninsula, setting up barriers in preparation for battle. The British ultimately won, but suffered such great losses they vowed to be more cautious in future battles.

Colonial citizens loyal to the crown resented the rebel insurrection and as many as 25,000 Loyalists joined the British army against the Continental Army.

The Second Continental Congress effectively became the government of the young nation, establishing its own army, negotiating treaties, and creating the official documents of the United Colonies. With increasing hostilities, it became clear that a negotiated peace was impossible with a tyrannical government which would only accept unconditional obedience.

TURNING POINTS

*B*oycotts and the destruction of shipments, like those with the Boston Tea Party, only made things worse for the colonies. When Massachusetts decided to create its own government parallel to that established by the crown, King George III considered the colony rebellious. The conflict escalated into armed violence.

Massachusetts was not alone in its resistance. Eleven other colonies joined the insurrection by establishing the Second Continental Congress and an army to protect colonial interests. By the time Georgia joined the other twelve, the last ditch attempt at peace had been sent to England.

PHILOSOPHICAL BASIS OF THE REVOLT

Subjects of the British Crown lived under an unwritten constitution that guaranteed certain rights and restrained the king from ruling by arbitrary edicts. Though not codified into written law until the 19th century, this constitution was a tacit understanding derived from five centuries of legal precedent. At the start of the 18th century, the 13

American colonies were sparsely populated, with about 250,000 people. Over the next several decades, the population grew to about 2.5 million. Thus, the American colonists represented 20% or more of the imperial population.

The implied contract between the government and the governed was broken when, after the Seven Years' War and its American portion (the French and Indian War), the British government began imposing taxes and arbitrary rules without giving the Americans a say in Parliament.

American resentment was based on the unequal treatment of English citizens and the lack of representation in Parliament. Moreover, the Americans began to become more critically aware of the nature and legitimacy of governments rather than merely taking their existence for granted. And in this new worldview, Americans began to see that a government by arbitrary rules was no longer one grounded in law but based on the whim of those in power.

All the perceived abuses suffered by the Americans between 1761 and 1775 were thus based on usurpation or theft of power by an arrogant few. Usurpation of power became a common theme in the arguments of America's Founding Fathers.

"A FREE people can never be too quick in observing, nor too firm in opposing the beginnings of alteration."

— *JOHN DICKINSON, 1767.*

At first, they sought to heal the wounds that had begun separating America from the motherland. When that failed, Americans — some reluctantly — began to consider a grand divorce between the home island and the continental colonies. Below is the full text of the *Declaration of Indepen-*

dence and commentary on the specific reasons for the intended split.

SIEGE AND LIBERATION OF BOSTON

By the end of autumn 1775, the Siege of Boston (April 19, 1775–March 17, 1776) had already lasted eight months. The conflict had reached a stalemate. General Washington sent Colonel Henry Knox in November to gain an advantage by retrieving heavy cannons from Fort Ticonderoga in upstate New York. The colonials captured the fort from the British six months earlier. Some of these armaments had greater range than anything previously available to the Americans.

Using sleds in an arduous path over land and across two major rivers, Knox secured some 60 tons of armaments. For the first few days of March 1776, the heavy artillery pieces were placed around the city to bombard British positions. These new armaments, however, did minor damage to the enemy.

On the night of March 5, 1776, General Washington had his men move many of the heavy cannons to Dorchester Heights, accompanied by several thousand soldiers. Because of the winter cold, the men could not easily dig trenches. Washington's forces constructed, out of view of the British, prefabricated defenses made of heavy timbers and other materials and put them into position overnight. Upon seeing the fortifications on the Heights, British General Howe reportedly said, "My God, these fellows have done more work in one night than I could make my army do in three months."

The Americans' clever position on Dorchester Heights proved unreachable by British cannon.

On March 8, Howe had some of the more well-known Bostonians send a message to Washington, informing him that they would not burn the city if the American general let the British withdraw unmolested.

By March 10, General Howe had prepared to evacuate Boston. He had ordered all citizens to give up their woolen and linen goods, which could help the rebel colonials through the war. Howe assigned Loyalist Crean Brush to receive the goods. British ships sat in Boston Harbor for a week, awaiting favorable winds. On March 17, by 9:00 a.m., all British ships were underway.

Though General Washington had not explicitly agreed to Howe's terms, the American general did allow the British to leave the city unmolested. However, he did not permit the British ships to depart the outer harbor without a fight. Several British ships were captured, including the one carrying Crean Brush and his linen and woolen plunder.

HOW THE SOUTH CHOSE SIDES

Many colonials of the southern states of Georgia, South Carolina, North Carolina, and Virginia recently arrived from Great Britain. In the region of North Carolina known as Cape Fear were settlers from the Highlands of Scotland. Along the southern coasts, many Anglicans lived who held resentment against the various colonial governments. These, the British leaders saw as remaining loyal to the British cause.

However, British leaders were wrong about the American South. Support for the crown was not as strong as they had hoped. Indeed, entire communities were torn between rebellion and acquiescence to British rule. In effect, the South became a quagmire resembling a Civil War with brother against brother.

You may remember that Georgia was the last of the thirteen colonies to join the First Continental Congress. So, after early failures in the South, the British concentrated their renewed efforts in the South on the Georgia colony's main seaport, Savannah, some two years later.

"Fear is the foundation of most governments."

— *JOHN ADAMS, LETTER TO GEORGE WYTHE,*
APRIL 1776.

BATTLE OF SULLIVAN'S ISLAND

Royal governors in the southern colonies sent word back to England that many Loyalists would be eager to restore order if only the British military were to show their support for such efforts. But the British governors in each colony, though they did not lie, exaggerated the degree of support British troops would enjoy in the South.

British forces abandoned Boston after the Battle of Bunker Hill and the liberation of Boston by the Americans. British leaders felt they would encounter far less resistance in the southern colonies. Also, the British economy depended heavily on the products made available by those colonies and the British West Indies, including rice, indigo, and tobacco.

Though British forces initially sought to attack North Carolina, they found conditions there unsuitable, so they regrouped and set sail for Charles Town, South Carolina (present-day Charleston).

Upon arriving, the British discovered that the Americans had begun to build a fort on Sullivan Island. At first, they deposited troops on nearby Long Island, hoping to attack the fort using ground forces. However, the channel between the two islands was too deep to allow the men to wade across.

On June 28, 1776, British forces opened fire upon Fort

Sullivan, using nine warships to bombard the fort with cannon and mortar fire. Over the next several hours, the flagship, Bristol, sent 1,840 cannon projectiles into the fort. But Fort Sullivan, using carefully aimed cannon, inflicted far more damage on the British ships. The Americans suffered only 12 killed and another 25 wounded, while the British casualties amounted to 93 killed and 127 wounded.

By the middle of the night, the British had decided that taking America's third-largest city was next to impossible for the time being.

DECLARATION OF INDEPENDENCE

"Our liberties do not come from charters; for these are only the declaration of pre-existing rights."

— *JOHN DICKINSON.*

On June 7, 1776, Richard Henry Lee offered a proposal for American independence. He would wait nearly a month before the Second Continental Congress adopted it.

Like his cousin, Sam, John Adams favored independence from Great Britain. After all, Massachusetts suffered greatly from the abuses of the British Empire. Understandably, so much British retribution against the colonies was aimed at Massachusetts. Still, so many other oppressive actions were indiscriminately aimed at all of the colonies, irrespective of their involvement in the resistance by Massachusetts.

By the late spring of 1776, it had become clear that England was not interested in reconciliation. Yet, on July 1, John Dickinson — one who still preferred some form of compromise — gave a lengthy speech (as much as 3 hours) to the Second Continental Congress against independence. He wished to try again to find some way to repair the rift between America and England.

John Dickinson of both Pennsylvania and Delaware was a cautious revolutionary. He was, after all, one of the chief architects of the *Declaration of the Causes* a year earlier, which had accompanied the *Olive Branch Petition*.

Even a year after Lexington, Concord, and Bunker Hill, Dickinson felt that the Adams cousins had been pushing too hard and fast. He felt there was still time to heal the wounds that damaged the relationship between the colonies and the empire.

When Dickinson had finished, the hall had become deathly quiet. The thoughts of those in attendance skirted around a most dangerous idea — that of independence. Their nervous silence dreaded the inevitable topic — one which would have to offer a counter-argument to that of Dickinson. But, at first, no one dared broach the subject, for if word ever made its way back to England, the person who had introduced the matter of separating from England would become labeled as a traitor to the crown and inevitably sentenced to death.

It did not take long for all eyes to turn toward John Adams; he had been a most energetic defender of liberty. But to risk discussing such a thing openly — in Congress — was to invite a death warrant.

John Adams stood and spoke for some 90 minutes — fiery arguments in favor of independence from the British Empire. Thomas Jefferson later described the speech as words that "moved us from our seats" and described Adams as "the Colossus of Independence." Another delegate described Adams as "the Atlas of Independence."

The following day, July 2, 1776, Congress voted for independence, adopting the Lee Resolution, offered nearly a month earlier, and immediately began drafting the document declaring that fact.

Adams recommended that Thomas Jefferson be the one to write the declaration document and a group of five Patriots assisted in developing its wording. The group of five included John Adams of Massachusetts, Benjamin Franklin of Pennsylvania, Thomas Jefferson of Virginia, Robert Livingston of New York, and Roger Sherman of Connecticut.

In the original draft of the Declaration, Thomas Jefferson wrote concerning King George III:

> *"[H]e has erected a multitude of new offices by a self-assumed power, & sent hither swarms of officers to harrass our people & eat out their substance . . . ."*

> — *THOMAS JEFFERSON, JULY 1776.*

The following is the text of the Declaration of Independence using the punctuation, spelling, capitalization, and wording of the copy on display at the National Archives Museum's Rotunda. The words in **bold italic** inserted within the document's body have been added as commentary.

IN CONGRESS, JULY 4, 1776

The unanimous Declaration of the thirteen united States of America, When in the Course of human events, it becomes necessary for one people to dissolve the political bands which have connected them with another, and to assume among the powers of the earth, the separate and equal station to which the Laws of Nature and of Nature's God entitle them, a decent respect to the opinions of mankind requires that they should declare the causes which impel them to the separation.

We hold these truths to be self-evident, that all men are created equal, that they are endowed by their Creator with certain unalienable Rights, that among these are Life, Liberty and the pursuit of Happiness.—That to secure these rights, Governments are instituted among Men, deriving their just powers from the consent of the governed, —That whenever any Form of Government becomes destructive of these ends, it is the Right of the People to alter or to abolish it, and to institute new Government, laying its foundation on such principles and organizing its powers in such form, as to them shall seem most likely to effect their Safety and Happiness.

The Declaration begins by establishing that people enjoy pre-existing rights and status that flow from Nature and God rather from government. Until this time, rulers had governed from the standpoint that their power was absolute — even godlike. Here, a new philosophy is established which puts any and all governments as servants of the people.

Prudence, indeed, will dictate that Governments long established should not be changed for light and transient causes; and accordingly all experience hath shewn, that mankind are more disposed to suffer, while evils are suffer-able, than to right themselves by abolishing the forms to which they are accustomed. But when a long train of abuses and usurpations, pursuing invariably the same Object evinces a design to reduce them under absolute Despotism, it is their right, it is their duty, to throw off such Government, and to provide new Guards for their future security.—Such has been the patient sufferance of these Colonies; and such is now the necessity which constrains them to alter their former Systems of Government. The history of the present King of Great Britain is a history of repeated injuries and usurpations, all having in direct object the establishment of an absolute Tyranny over these States. To prove this, let Facts be submitted to a candid world.

The Declaration uses the words "tyranny" and "usurpation," indicating the nature of the king's arbitrary edicts taking on powers which do not belong to him. And the examples of these thefts of power committed by the king and his Parliament make up the following list, many of which echo the circumstances surrounding the various Acts described in Chapter 1 above, "Uprising."

•He has refused his Assent to Laws, the most wholesome and necessary for the public good.

•He has forbidden his Governors to pass Laws of immediate and pressing importance, unless suspended in their operation till his Assent should be obtained; and when so suspended, he has utterly neglected to attend to them.

•He has refused to pass other Laws for the accommodation of large districts of people, unless those people would relinquish the right of Representation in the Legislature, a right inestimable to them and formidable to tyrants only.

•He has called together legislative bodies at places unusual, uncomfortable, and distant from the depository of their public Records, for the sole purpose of fatiguing them into compliance with his measures.

•He has dissolved Representative Houses repeatedly, for opposing with manly firmness his invasions on the rights of the people.

•He has refused for a long time, after such dissolutions, to cause others to be elected; whereby the Legislative powers, incapable of Annihilation, have returned to the People at large for their exercise; the State remaining in the mean time exposed to all the dangers of invasion from without, and convulsions within.

•He has endeavoured to prevent the population of these States; for that purpose obstructing the Laws for Naturalization of Foreigners; refusing to pass others to encourage their migrations hither, and raising the conditions of new Appropriations of Lands.

•He has obstructed the Administration of Justice, by refusing his Assent to Laws for establishing Judiciary powers.

•He has made Judges dependent on his Will alone, for the tenure of their offices, and the amount and payment of their salaries.

•He has erected a multitude of New Offices, and sent hither swarms of Officers to harrass our people, and eat out their substance.

•He has kept among us, in times of peace, Standing Armies without the Consent of our legislatures.

•He has affected to render the Military independent of and superior to the Civil power.

•He has combined with others to subject us to a jurisdiction foreign to our constitution, and unacknowledged by our laws; giving his Assent to their Acts of pretended Legislation:

•For Quartering large bodies of armed troops among us:

•For protecting them, by a mock Trial, from punishment for any Murders which they should commit on the Inhabitants of these States:

•For cutting off our Trade with all parts of the world:

•For imposing Taxes on us without our Consent:

•For depriving us in many cases, of the benefits of Trial by Jury:

•For transporting us beyond Seas to be tried for pretended offences

•For abolishing the free System of English Laws in a neighbouring Province, establishing therein an Arbitrary government, and enlarging its Boundaries so as to render it at once an example and fit instrument for introducing the same absolute rule into these Colonies:

•For taking away our Charters, abolishing our most valuable Laws, and altering fundamentally the Forms of our Governments:

•For suspending our own Legislatures, and declaring themselves invested with power to legislate for us in all cases whatsoever.

•He has abdicated Government here, by declaring us out of his Protection and waging War against us.

•He has plundered our seas, ravaged our Coasts, burnt our towns, and destroyed the lives of our people.

•He is at this time transporting large Armies of foreign Mercenaries to compleat the works of death, desolation and tyranny, already begun with circumstances of Cruelty & perfidy scarcely paralleled in the most barbarous ages, and totally unworthy the Head of a civilized nation.

•He has constrained our fellow Citizens taken Captive on the high Seas to bear Arms against their Country, to become the executioners of their friends and Brethren, or to fall themselves by their Hands.

•He has excited domestic insurrections amongst us, and has endeavoured to bring on the inhabitants of our frontiers, the merciless Indian Savages, whose known rule of warfare, is an undistinguished destruction of all ages, sexes and conditions.

In every stage of these Oppressions We have Petitioned for Redress in the most humble terms: Our repeated Petitions have been answered only by repeated injury. A Prince whose character is thus marked by every act which may define a Tyrant, is unfit to be the ruler of a free people.

Nor have We been wanting in attentions to our British brethren. We have warned them from time to time of attempts by their legislature to extend an unwarrantable jurisdiction over us. We have reminded them of the circumstances of our emigration and settlement here. We have appealed to their native justice and magnanimity, and we have conjured them by the ties of our common kindred to disavow these usurpations, which, would inevitably interrupt our connections and correspondence. They too have been deaf to the voice of justice and of consanguinity. We must, therefore, acquiesce in the necessity, which denounces our Separation, and hold them, as we hold the rest of mankind, Enemies in War, in Peace Friends.

We, therefore, the Representatives of the united States of America, in General Congress, Assembled, appealing to the Supreme Judge of the world for the rectitude of our intentions, do, in the Name, and by Authority of the good People of these Colonies, solemnly publish and declare, That these United Colonies are, and of Right ought to be Free and Independent States; that they are Absolved from all Allegiance to the British Crown, and that all political connection between them and the State of Great Britain, is and ought to be totally dissolved; and that as Free and Independent States, they have full Power to levy War, conclude Peace, contract Alliances, establish Commerce, and to do all other Acts and Things which Independent States may of right do. And for the support of this Declaration, with a firm reliance on the protection of divine Providence, we mutually pledge to each other our Lives, our Fortunes and our sacred Honor.

PATRIOT JOHN ADAMS

Of the most well known of America's Founding Fathers, George Washington and John Adams were the two who worked the hardest for their nation's independence.

During the next several months, John Adams served on 90 committees. Most importantly, Adams served as the Board of War and Ordinance president, so he ran the war's logistical side for independence. And, again, of all the key

Founding Fathers, no one was more intimately involved in the war for independence except for General George Washington.

It is no wonder that the first two presidents of these United States were George Washington, followed by John Adams.

BATTLE OF LONG ISLAND

After the liberation of Boston in March, General Washington suspected that the British would attack America's premier port city of New York, the largest city in the American colonies with a population of approximately 25,000. He moved his troops there and set up to protect the city from attack.

In the meantime, British General Howe withdrew his forces to British-held Halifax, Nova Scotia. This allowed them time to regain strength after their short rations in Boston.

British leaders felt they would find more Loyalists in New York than Boston. By taking America's principal seaport and thus controlling the Hudson River, which led north from it, they would have split the colonies. Then, with forces from Canada, they could put down the rebellion in the "New England" colonies, thus leaving only the southern colonies to deal with.

As Washington established his forces toward the western end of Long Island, he sent spies to keep an eye on the British military installations, which were already there. One of those spies was a man named Nathan Hale, pretending to be a Dutch teacher. The British uncovered his role as a spy and had him hanged. The young man's last words became a famous rallying cry for all Patriots: "I only regret that I have but one life to lose for my country."

Washington expected a naval attack and built up his defenses accordingly. He had his men build seven forts in the Brooklyn area, some overlooking the waters leading toward Manhattan and the East River. He also set up in lower Manhattan an array of artillery. Forts included,

- Fort Box,
- Fort Corkscrew (Cobble Hill),
- Fort Defiance,
- Fort Greene,
- Fort Putnam, and
- Fort Stirling.

American forces had about 30 cannons facing the water among the several forts.

On July 2, the same day Congress discussed independence, the British fleet showed up with 130 ships with a complement of roughly 9,000 troops. Their forces set up camp on Staten Island across from the city. A week later, General Howe's brother, Admiral Richard Howe, arrived with 150 additional ships and 13,000 more troops. As the naval reinforcements continued to reach New York into August, the total number of British ships had risen slightly more than 400.

Once the initial camp had been prepared, the British sent a negotiation team across Long Island to ask if Washington was ready to surrender, promising him a pardon from the king. The general replied, "Those who have committed no fault want no pardon."

On August 22, the British began transferring troops to Long Island in preparation for their assault on American forces. Washington had his men hold their defensive positions. In all, the British had about 20,000 men to Washington's 10,000. Of the British troops, about 9,000 were Hessians (German mercenaries).

Early on Tuesday, August 27, 1776, the British sent a

small force to engage the center of the American defensive line. While the Americans were preoccupied, the central portion of British troops attacked from the East, outflanking the Patriot forces.

Outnumbered, Washington pulled most of his men back to Brooklyn Heights, giving them the higher-ground advantage. Four hundred men of the Maryland militia stayed behind to protect the American withdrawal from other positions.

Remembering the fiasco at Bunker Hill, the British decided not to risk more of their soldiers' lives trying to finish off the Americans. In addition, it seemed that the American forces were trapped. Hence, the British generals were in no hurry to finish them off.

In the aftermath: Americans: 300 were killed, 800 wounded, 1,079 captured or missing. British: 64 killed, 293 wounded, 31 captured or missing.

On the night of August 29–30, Washington told his men to be as quiet as possible and to make their way under the full moon, in the fog and rain, across the East River to Manhattan Island. In the morning, the British discovered that the Americans had escaped.

RETREAT FROM NEW YORK

The Battle of Long Island had been a dismal defeat for Washington. He had come very close to losing the entire war in this one campaign to protect New York from falling into British hands. General Washington had orders from Congress and did his best over the following two months to keep the city out of British hands.

For two weeks, General William Howe did not pursue Washington. In that period of relative peace, on September 11, 1776, three men from the Second Continental Congress

— the ruling body for the former American British colonies — met at the home of a Loyalist on Staten Island near New York. These men were Edward Rutledge, John Adams, and Benjamin Franklin. This was supposed to have been a peace conference. Still, the British side demanded that the Americans submit to the supremacy of the English Parliament over the American Congress as a condition for starting peace negotiations. The British agents had not yet learned to understand the American position. The talks were perfunctory.

New York was what we consider in 21st-century America a moderately small town of about 25,000 people. That covered the lower end of Manhattan. On September 12, 1776, a war council decided to abandon New York and move the focus of defense farther north to Harlem Heights.

On September 15, British General Howe placed 4,000 soldiers on Manhattan Island at Kip's Bay. Americans defending there lost their resolve and proved incompetent against the advancing British.

The following day, British forces added insult to the previous day's injury by having their buglers use their horns in "the manner of a fox chase." The small force of American soldiers understood the insult all too well and mustered the courage to rout a British light infantry detachment. This became known as the Battle of Harlem Heights.

Five days later, a fire consumed more than a thousand buildings from St. Paul's Chapel to Bowling Green. This did not help either side of the conflict. The Americans, of course, did not want American property destroyed. The British, naturally, wanting to capture the city, wanted this to be a city after its capture instead of a burnt-out wilderness.

Through a series of losses, by the end of October 1776, the Continental Army had effectively lost most of the New York area to the British, except for Fort Washington on

Manhattan opposite the river from Fort Lee in New Jersey. The two acted as an effective barrier to British ships which might want to sail farther north on the Hudson River. A series of British assaults on the fort resulted in its capture on November 16, 1776. The capture proved to be a major blow to the American cause, with the loss of 2,800 men — killed or captured — and the loss of a strategic fort.

Washington had moved his remaining forces to Fort Lee in New Jersey in full view of the garrison's fall at Fort Washington.

Throughout the remainder of the war, New York stayed in British hands, a permanent reminder of the early losses in the Americans' desperate attempt at liberty.

Winter weather closed off virtually all war efforts, giving both sides time to reflect and plan.

> *'These are the times that try men's souls . . . . Britain, with an army to enforce her tyranny, has declared that she has a right (not only to TAX) but 'to BIND us in ALL CASES WHATSOEV-ER,' and if being bound in that manner, is not slavery, then is there not such a thing as slavery upon earth. Even the expression is impious; for so unlimited a power can belong only to God."*

> — *THOMAS PAINE, DECEMBER 19, 1776, THE AMERICAN CRISIS, PAMPHLET SERIES #1.*

In one of Thomas Paine's more famous writings, the words of the *Declaratory Act of 1766* a decade earlier return to remind Americans of the desperate need to throw off the British yoke, for the crown and its government had made clear their intention to treat the Americans as third-class citizens — lower even than the commoners of England.

With the loss of New York City, General George Washington had failed in a primary mission. Because of this, Washington's reputation had been significantly weakened in the eyes of his fellow Americans and those of other nations looking on at the harrowing conflict.

THREAT FROM CANADA

In 1775, the population of Lower Canada (Quebec) was about 96,000. They consisted mainly of French-speaking, British, Catholic subjects after France lost Canada to Great Britain due to the Seven Years' War (French and Indian War in North America). The province of Nova Scotia, consisting of modern-day Nova Scotia, Prince Edward Island, and Newfoundland, had a total population of about 46,000. These posed a threat from the North to the most northern of the thirteen colonies in rebellion — a region commonly known even today as New England.

After open warfare had erupted in Massachusetts, the United Colonies discussed the potential threat from Canada — most notably from the part known as Quebec. But what if Quebec could become the 14th colony in rebellion against England? Co-opting Quebec would require the British military presence in Quebec to be eliminated, and the French Canadians become convinced to join the United Colonies' effort. And because most British troops in the Americas had been trapped in Boston, the American Patriots favored an attack on Quebec.

With this in mind, American General Richard Montgomery gathered 1,200 men on August 25, 1775, at Fort Ticonderoga, a military installation recently captured from the British. From there, they marched northward from the New York colony into Quebec.

Between September 17 and November 3, Montgomery laid siege against Fort Saint-Jean in southern Quebec. On

October 30, the British governor of Quebec, General Sir Guy Carleton, attempted to stop the siege but failed. By November 3, the officers in charge of the fort chose to surrender. After that success, Montgomery had his men invade Montreal, which Carleton had abandoned as indefensible. Offering no resistance, the city surrendered to General Montgomery on November 13, 1775.

The Continental Army's new commander-in-chief, George Washington, ordered a second phase of the attack. The general sent Colonel Benedict Arnold with 1,100 men through the backcountry of the northern colonies to assist General Montgomery. The rugged, nearly uninhabited terrain proved too much for Arnold's contingent. Roughly a hundred men died, and another 400 deserted. Arnold's remaining men reached Quebec City on November 14, 1775, awaiting the arrival of reinforcements from General Montgomery.

When Montgomery arrived on December 2, the combined forces numbered roughly 1,100 men. By December 5, the United Colonies' men were ready to engage the British.

At the end of December, Montgomery devised a plan which he was sure would result in the surrender of Quebec City. Three divisions, one each under the commands of General Montgomery, Colonel Arnold, and Colonel James Livingston, attacked the city from different directions. However, a growing snowstorm made it more difficult for the United Colonies soldiers, most notably because the snow made it virtually impossible to fire their muskets. The battle left Montgomery dead, and Arnold wounded.

Arnold assumed command but remained unable to accomplish what his commander had failed to do.

By May 1776, British General John Burgoyne had arrived at Quebec City with reinforcements, forcing

Colonel Arnold and his men to retreat to the New York colony.

Congress wanted an explanation for the failure in Quebec. Some delegates pointed to the outbreak of smallpox, which had weakened their men. Others pointed to the ill-timed snowstorm. Ultimately, however, Congress determined that the failure was a fault of their mismanagement. They felt that more resources and a more aggressive strategy could have won Quebec as a 14th colony for their cause. This popular sentiment would remain in American politics for decades, even into the War of 1812, when a similar military campaign failed to wrest Quebec from the British.

BATTLES OF TRENTON & PRINCETON

Washington had lost New York! After several defeats, he failed in that vital mission, which forced him to retreat into Pennsylvania. The general was determined to end the first full year of war with a win. General Washington was determined not to be defined by the setbacks in the New York colony. Indeed, as Thomas Paine so poignantly wrote, these were the times that try men's souls and force them to reflect deeply on the direction they would take in life.

The Delaware River, which marks the entire western border of New Jersey, separated that smaller colony from Pennsylvania. Along the eastern seaboard of what is now these United States, the Delaware is the longest river, with sources in the region of the New York colony. Washington would need to cross the Delaware to engage with the British forces. They had stopped their pursuit of the Americans because of the coming winter and because Washington had, near the point of crossing, removed all boats from the New Jersey shore to the Pennsylvania side of the river.

From December 20th through 24th, 1776, Washington

received reinforcements, and on Christmas Eve, received much-needed provisions and blankets. Some of his troops were immediately assigned to guard strategic locations.

Preparations for crossing into New Jersey began on December 23, and by late afternoon Christmas Day, General George Washington told 2,400 of his men to prepare for a secret mission. They were taking horses, cannons, and provisions. A veritable flotilla was prepared for them.

Conditions were nasty — cold, winter wind with rain which turned into snow as temperatures dropped. Ice formed on the river, making it difficult for the artillery to cross until about 3 a.m. By 4 a.m., however, the men were ready to march.

British General Cornwallis had placed Hessian auxiliary troops in Trenton and several other outposts along the western New Jersey border. The Hessian troops were from the region known today as Germany. King George III's family was from Germany. While George III was king of Great Britain, he was also Duke and Prince-elector of the Hanover region of Brunswick-Lüneburg in the Holy Roman Empire. In 1814, King George III also gained the title of King of Hanover, which heightened the conflicts of interest in this monarch who oversaw two kingdoms.

Washington ordered General Sullivan, with half the men, to march down River Road. At the same time, Washington and General Greene would travel with the other half of their attack force along a parallel road farther inland.

Hours earlier, on Christmas night, Trenton's postmaster, Abraham Hunt, played the part of a Loyalist and host to British Colonel Rall and his men, plying them with food and drink. With the harsh weather and the welcoming accommodations of Postmaster Hunt, Rall needed to prepare to respond to Washington's sudden surprise attack.

Startled and unprepared, the Hessians and their

commander surrendered. Only 3 Americans had been killed, with six wounded, while 22 Hessians were killed and 98 of the British auxiliary forces were wounded. Rall was wounded and soon died. The Americans took 1,000 prisoners from the Trenton raid, plus artillery, powder, and muskets. One young officer — a fellow Virginian, James Monroe, nearly died from the wounds he sustained during the battle. Washington promoted him to captain following the surprise Trenton attack. Monroe later became the fifth president of these United States.

Colonel John Cadwalader had discovered that most British forces in New Jersey had been moved northward to the region of Princeton. Washington's war council recommended attacking the British at Princeton to magnify their recent win.

To accomplish this, Washington would need to use most of his army, leaving very few of them to guard positions in Pennsylvania. Washington was prepared to take this calculated risk; few British were brazen enough to attack in such dark weather. Because of the immense undertaking, eight separate crossing points were used. At some locations, the ice was thick enough for men to cross on foot.

But Washington faced another problem as the year ended and the preparations were being finalized. Many of his men had expiring enlistments. They would no longer be bound to fight unless the General could convince them to reenlist for a few more weeks. Washington accomplished this by promising funds from the Continental Congress.

On New Year's Day, 1777, money arrived from Congress, and Washington paid his men. In the meantime, Washington had learned that British forces were moving from Princeton to Trenton under General Cornwallis.

On January 2, 1777, George Washington was again near Trenton, across Assunpink Creek from the town. There,

Washington won the second strategic battle of Trenton and pushed on toward Princeton in the dead of night. Cornwallis was left bewildered at how these Americans had fooled him.

Cornwallis had moved some 8,000 troops out of Princeton, leaving 1,400 behind under Colonel Mawhood. This would prove to be a mistake. By British standards, the loss in New Jersey was only a minor defeat. Still, it significantly boosted the morale of the American troops and officers.

Brigadier General Hugh Mercer and his Patriot men were the first to engage with Mawhood. Still, the Americans were ill-equipped and were overrun by British forces. Cadwalader attacked, followed by Washington, and forced Mawhood to surrender.

In all, 4,500 Americans, with 35 cannons, fought against 1,200 British, with as many as nine cannons. Roughly 40 Americans were killed and 40 wounded, while about 80 British were killed and 65 wounded, with about 240 captured.

Afterward, Washington and his men sought winter quarters to wait for spring. With these two key victories, Washington regained much of his reputation. It restored some faith in him for conducting the war of independence.

TEST YOUR UNDERSTANDING

Answers to the following questions may be found in the Appendix.

1. What was part of the basis for American resentment against Great Britain?

•An inability to get good tea in America.

•Unequal treatment of English citizens.

•Colonists were not given adequate protection from indigenous tribes and the French.

•All of the above.

2. How did the Patriots gain the upper hand in the Siege of Boston?

•Siege cannon manufactured locally by American craftsmen.

•A new design of siege cannon invented by an American manufacturer.

•A more significant number of siege cannons arrayed against the British.

•Larger cannon transported from Ticonderoga.

3. What blunder in planning did the British make about their war against the Americans?

•Assuming that Loyalist support in the South was strong.

•Assuming that their larger and more experienced military was all they needed to win.

•Assuming that the inexperienced local militias were no match for the seasoned British Red Coats.

•All of the above.

4. Who is credited with saying the famous line, "I only regret that I have but one life to lose for my country"?

•General George Washington

•Colonel Benedict Arnold

•Lieutenant James Monroe

•First Lieutenant Nathan Hale

5. What problem jeopardized Washington's crossing the Delaware River to launch a surprise attack on the British?

•Ice too thick on the river.

•Enlistments were expiring.

•A British spy in his ranks.

•Low on ammunition.

SUMMING IT UP

American colonists felt cheated out of their English birthright. They felt as though they were treated as third-class citizens or worse. The Americans saw the abuses they suffered as an extension of the British government's usurpation of powers beyond those legitimately belonging to them.

After nearly a year of laying siege to Boston, the Patriots successfully expelled the British after securing more powerful cannons from Fort Ticonderoga.

With the center of rebellion seeming to reside in the northern colonies, the British, on the advice of southern governors, decided to focus their efforts on a Southern Solution, first attempting to take Charleston, South Carolina, on June 28, 1776. Their attempt in the second year of the war failed.

Meanwhile, the Patriot leaders finally decided to break with the Empire at the Second Continental Congress. They drafted one of the most famous documents of all time — the *Declaration of Independence*, completed and approved on July 4, 1776.

The early success of the Patriots in Boston made the British more cautious. Congress instructed General Washington to hold New York City against all British assaults. But the British, with as many as 400 ships carrying troops, had roughly twice as many men as Washington. Over the next several weeks of fighting, Washington and the Continental Army were forced to retreat from New York, and the city remained in British hands until after the end of the war.

American Patriots came up with the wild idea that Quebec might be added as a 14th colony to their efforts for independence. After nearly a year of action, however, the American assault failed.

Desperate to regain some dignity after the massive failure at New York, General Washington devised a bold attack during the brutal cold of winter. Twice, he took his men east across the Delaware River, from Pennsylvania into New

Jersey, and successfully attacked the British at Trenton and then Princeton.

Washington had no way of knowing how long the war would last. Still, he knew he needed to keep the fight alive long enough for the American diplomats to gain support from the enemies of Great Britain.

STRUGGLES, SETBACKS, AND SUPPORT

*W*inter during the Little Ice Age (1350–1850) brought a far more bitter cold than in our Modern Warm Period (1850–present). In British history, the Thames River in London has frozen over only rarely since the early 19th century. But as late as 1814, that English river had ice thick enough to support fairs and even elephants! Similarly, cold weather gripped the American countryside throughout the Revolutionary War.

Such a brutal cold makes war a far more demanding activity. One aspect of that difficulty involves finding food for warriors and their horses.

THE FORAGE WAR

Right after the Battle of Princeton, about 20 American militia on horseback captured a supply train filled with winter clothing, all of which the Patriots put to good use. General Washington ordered the men under his command to clear the region of all cattle and other potential foraging resources so that the British would have a more challenging time surviving the winter. This forced British foraging parties to cover more extensive territories, making them more vulnerable to attack.

Washington's forces had been reduced to about 2,500 men as terms of enlistment began to expire. But the early successes of the Forage War triggered the voluntary aid of more and more local militiamen.

The cocksure British thought they could put down the local revolts with a show of force, but their plan backfired when their German infantrymen were caught or killed. Very few of the British cavalrymen escaped to tell of their losses.

By the spring of 1777, British General Howe was anxious to reestablish control over the disruptive colonies.

BURGOYNE'S OFFENSIVE

After the British loss at Bunker Hill in 1776 and the successes of Washington at Trenton and Princeton, British leaders realized they needed a more coordinated attack against these unruly colonials. Colonial Secretary of State, Lord George Germain, wanted a plan to produce wins for the Empire against the rebels.

General Sir John Burgoyne, second to General Sir Guy Carleton in Canada, offered a proposal to gain a win for the British and to advance his position within the military. He proposed that he lead a two-part attack against Albany, New York. Part of his plan included a small amount of support from British General Howe, who was stationed in New York City.

General Howe offered his plan, which included attacks against the colonial capital, Philadelphia, plus efforts against both Albany and Boston.

Both generals felt they could quell the colonial uprising by year's end. Germain approved both plans.

THE BRITISH IN NEW YORK

Following the fall of New York on November 16, 1776, the British held America's largest city for the remaining seven years of the war. Whenever the rebels had a victory in surrounding regions, more Loyalists would flee to New York to escape the potential threats from these American traitors to the Empire and to seek refuge amongst the forces of the crown. Thus, the entire New York colony became increasingly more concentrated, with citizens who wanted no part in the push for independence.

Yet, the two armies — British and American — needed supplies. Enterprising locals would smuggle goods across the river to earn a living.

British officials made it known that slaves would be set free if they joined the British effort. These and similar incentives made managing the war an increasingly complex affair. General Washington even corresponded with New York Governor George Clinton about such issues.

F.P. Mann, in a 2013 dissertation on the British occupation, wrote, "While it is virtually inevitable that a military occupation will be unpleasant for the inhabitants, some occupations may be worse than others. In a colonial rebellion, regaining the hearts and minds, the love and loyalty of the populace is vital. Therefore, it is imperative that the occupiers from the mother country try to minimize objectionable or appalling incidents with the occupied population and protect the people from criminals or raids. A violent or even ineffectual occupation could poison the effort to restore a colonial region to the empire." So, the British commanders also had many challenges maintaining the morale of their men, feeding and lodging them, finding wood for fires to keep them warm and to cook their meals, and keeping the men from straying too far from duty and discipline.

When George Washington finally returned to New York City seven years and six days after his forces were defeated there, he took Governor Clinton of New York with him. Together, they would have to figure out what to do with the Loyalists and the former slaves who had enlisted in the British army.

THE BATTLES OF SARATOGA

British General Burgoyne moved his forces — over 7,000 men, including several Hessians, plus a large party of Native Americans — along Lake Champlain on June 18, 1777, and reached the vicinity of Ft. Ticonderoga, which the Americans had captured early in the war. By July 6, Burgoyne had retaken the fort and its surrounding defenses.

Because of the loss of Ticonderoga, the American government replaced General Philip Schuyler with General Horatio Gates as commander of the Northern Department. Upon learning of Burgoyne's advances, Washington sent General Benedict Arnold and General Benjamin Lincoln to assist.

General Barry St. Leger moved in from the West with a motley assortment of British regulars, Loyalists, French Canadiens, and Native Americans. He found the defenses at Fort Stanwix (the modern city of Rome, New York) too strong to overcome. He laid siege against the fort throughout much of August. When the fort was about to receive reinforcements, his Native American contingent fled, leaving him undermanned. Because of these failures, St. Leger never made it to Saratoga to assist Burgoyne and was forced to retreat.

Along the Hudson River, Saratoga is about 30 miles (48 kilometers) north of Albany — Burgoyne's destination. And because of the rough terrain on either side of the river valley, any heavily equipped army would find it next to impossible to travel anywhere other than the valley itself. This made the confrontation between British and American forces unavoidable.

In the meantime, General Howe pursued his passion for capturing Philadelphia instead of more fully supporting Burgoyne's campaign. Howe left General Sir Henry Clinton in charge of New York with instructions to assist Burgoyne if the prospect seemed favorable or necessary.

On August 28, Burgoyne learned that St. Leger had been turned back at Ft. Stanwix, so now he knew he would not receive reinforcements from the West.

Burgoyne felt that maintaining communication with the North was consuming too many resources, so he ordered his men to abandon the outposts between Saratoga and Ft. Ticonderoga. He was becoming increasingly concerned about the upcoming change in seasons. Either Burgoyne would need to find winter quarters in Ticonderoga or Albany; he chose the latter. Between September 13th and 15th, he had his men cross the Hudson River to its western shores.

After having lost his Native American support, Burgoyne became even more cautious. He moved his forces south toward Albany, but the leading edge of his army met with some resistance from American scouting parties on September 18.

On September 19, 1777, General Burgoyne's forces met the Americans at Freeman's Farm, about 10 miles (16 kilometers) south of Saratoga. By some estimates, the American forces stood at about 9,000 compared to the British 7,200. Even so, the British won the day, but with significant losses.

Rather than attack the Americans again, Burgoyne regrouped and allowed his men to collect their dead.

On October 7, the second battle began with 6,600 British and German soldiers facing about 12,000 Americans. By the time of Burgoyne's surrender, the American side had gained another 3,000 men.

General Clinton sailed up the Hudson River on October 3, 1777, with roughly 3,000 men to assist in Burgoyne's offensive, but it was too late. Clinton's forces only made it as far north as Kingston, New York, about 69 miles (111 kilometers) south of the final battle, and only on October 13, 1777 — nearly a week after Burgoyne's surrender.

Ultimately, American losses amounted to 90 killed and 240 wounded, while the British had 440 killed, 695 wounded, and 6,222 captured.

Saratoga was the first significant win of the entire war and a sufficient victory for foreign leaders to look favorably upon the American cause for liberty.

TREATMENT OF PRISONERS OF WAR (POWS)

When King George III declared in 1775 that the Americans were traitors, that automatically denied any Americans captured the status as official prisoners-of-war (POWs). Such status generally afforded more humane treatment for soldiers and officers, but this only worked for prisoners of a foreign, sovereign power. In the minds of the British aristocracy, the Americans did not fit that description.

Even so, the British were reticent to apply the full force of this for fear that they would lose some much-needed support amongst the Loyalists. If the British had arrested, tried, and hanged every traitor they captured, they could easily have lost the hearts of thousands who might have been borderline Loyalists. Not hanging the traitors was part of a cunning strategy to win the hearts of more Americans by seeming at least moderately reasonable in their tyranny.

But hanging was hardly necessary when thousands died from the bleak conditions in prison.

When word of poor prisoner treatment got back to the Patriots who were not directly involved in the war, this spotlighted the differences between the "savage Britons" and the patriotic Americans. The harrowing stories of prisoners found their way into broadsides and newspapers, inflaming the passions of Americans ever more fervently to see their cause through to the end.

But the Americans' treatment of the British and Loyalist prisoners was sometimes just as cruel as that of the American Patriots by the British. Each side felt justified in mistreating prisoners, who were viewed as traitors or tyrants.

In the 18th century, prison conditions were invariably unhealthy and frequently inhumane. Though certain customs had come into use concerning the treatment of prisoners, no law held these customs in place. While officers were given preferential treatment, common soldiers had to endure harsher conditions and more significant restrictions. However, the accepted customs did not apply to the American rebellion, for America was not considered a sovereign body but a rebellious part of the British Empire.

After General Washington had been defeated on Long Island in 1776, a few thousand militiamen and regular troops had been taken as prisoners of war. Many were held in warehouses in the city or on damaged or captured ships, turned into prisons, and anchored in the harbor. Conditions were cramped and fraught with disease and vermin. As many as 11,000 prisoners died from the harsh conditions. In large part, the deaths were more a product of poor planning and a lack of resources rather than malice. Early in the war, Washington had warned British General Gage about the mistreatment of prisoners, intending to jog his memory that the "Obligation arising from the Rights of Humanity, and claims of Rank are universally binding, and extensive," but felt compelled to add, "except in case of Retaliation." This last phrase was a warning that the behavior of the British toward the American POWs could be reflected in the American treatment of the British. One can only wonder why the British dismissed the possibility that any of their men or officers would ever be captured.

However, the British policy of harsh prisoner treatment changed after the loss at Saratoga. Because so many officers and soldiers had been captured by the Americans, the British feared revenge by the colonial rebels. The former arrogance and dismissal by the British of American demands for fair treatment suddenly softened when their men were at risk of the same treatment.

Late in the war, the threat of reprisals in the treatment of POWs led officers on both sides of the conflict to seek an accord and prisoner exchange. And this recognition by the British of American soldiers and militia as official prisoners of war became a powerful statement that legitimized the American struggle for independence.

EUROPEAN ASSISTANCE

While the British received aid from the German Hessians and other German mercenaries, because of King George III's ties and loyalties to one of the numerous Germanic states, Americans sought the help of other European nations that were enemies of Great Britain.

Throughout most of 1777, the potential sources of aid were reticent to commit to any form of support. After news of the American success at Saratoga, New York, the nations of France, Spain, and the Netherlands felt satisfied that the Americans could succeed in their revolt. And who can blame them? Wars are expensive, and they did not want to waste their investment on a losing proposition.

REASONS FOR ASSISTANCE

There were many reasons why another nation would risk helping the Americans win their freedom. Primary amongst these was the preexisting enmity between their nation and Great Britain. For example, the French and the Spanish had lost a massive war to England a little over a decade earlier. That was the Seven Years' War — perhaps the world's first truly global war. The Netherlands had also fought in the past against Great Britain. So, revenge and prestige were two motives that drove those nations to support the American cause.

Great Britain had become the supreme power in the world and, in doing so, had made enemies of many of the other nations in Europe. By helping the Americans, they were actively opposing their enemy.

America's allies also hoped to reclaim some of the land they had lost to the British. In addition, they would enjoy trade with a new economic partner — these United States.

Although perhaps a lesser motivation, the freedom these Americans sought was an inspiration to some of the other peoples of Europe. Indeed they thought of Great Britain as evil, and freedom from that tyranny would be good in and of itself. Still, the notion of broader freedom may have stimulated the imagination of others to wish the Americans great success.

INTERNATIONAL DIPLOMACY

With the need for international diplomacy keen in their minds, the Continental Congress sought to create a template for the treaties they would be using. John Adams created what has been cited as the model for all future treaties based on the premise that America, under normal circumstances, should never have entangling alliances. Of course, fighting Great Britain was anything but ordinary.

Once Congress had formally declared independence, they sent a delegation to France led by Benjamin Franklin. Their mission was to secure an alliance with France.

When news of the British evacuation of Boston had made its way to France, the French foreign minister, M. Comte de Vergennes, favored an alliance. But before he could implement that alliance, he also heard of Washington's horrible Long Island and New York defeats. Suddenly, an alliance did not seem like such a wise idea.

Of course, everyone in Europe had heard of the fabulous Mr. Franklin, who had snatched electricity from the sky. At a stately 71 years of age, Franklin was in his element as a consummate diplomat, and the French had gone wild for everything American. They loved the honesty and simplicity of the republican ideal, an inspiration he cultivated. This helped Vergennes push through a loan to the United States in secret.

Even with the loan, France wanted to commit itself openly to the American cause if it had greater assurances of victory. To that end, Vergennes contacted the Spanish to entice them to join in the attacks on the British. However, Spain wanted to know if they could regain lost territories if they helped in the American effort.

At the end of 1777, Vergennes learned of the British defeat at Saratoga. This American success was all he needed to recommend to the court of 23-year-old King Louis XVI that they should openly ally France with the Americans. Not waiting for the Spanish, France offered a full alliance. Benjamin Franklin and two of his commissioners — Silas Deane and Arthur Lee — signed the Treaty of Alliance and the Treaty of Amity and Commerce with France on February 6, 1778.

SUPPORT FOR THE AMERICAN CAUSE

Later, on June 21, 1779, Spain joined the Franco-American alliance. Not only did they send supplies, but their forces attacked British-held forts in Alabama, Florida, and Mississippi.

While the Netherlands made loans to America, other nations like Denmark, Norway, Portugal, and Russia aided the Americans differently.

From this alliance, the French supplied to the Americans, from 1778 to 1782, all manner of aid: uniforms, shoes, and other clothing for the American troops; weapons, gunpowder, and ammunition; military officers and additional troops; and naval support in fighting off the British fleet, harassing their every move to protect Washington's forces. One of those officers was Marquis de Lafayette.

After the British surrender at Yorktown in 1781, the Americans sought and received the consent of Vergennes to begin peace negotiations with the British. Despite numerous attempts by the British to pit the allies against one another, they remained a unified front during their negotiations for peace. The war was formally ended with the Treaty of Paris in 1783.

JOHN ADAMS, TIRELESS PATRIOT FOR THE REVOLUTION

In November 1777, John Adams was selected to help enlist the aid of France in battling the British. He was appointed to replace Silas Deane and to join Ben Franklin and Arthur Lee in Paris.

On February 17, 1778, Adams, with his 10-year-old son, John Quincy Adams, set sail on the frigate *Boston*. While crossing the Atlantic, the ship encountered a major storm.

Lightning injured 19 sailors and killed one other. Later, John Adams took up arms to help capture one of the British ships pursuing them. This was still the Little Ice Age, and violent storms were more frequent during that era than today. Both John Adams and John Quincy Adams were to become future presidents.

When the ship arrived in France on April 1, 1778, Adams learned that a treaty had already been signed several weeks earlier, on February 6—some 11 days before he had left America.

In a message received in September 1778, Congress increased Franklin's powers of negotiation and sent Lee to Spain. With no instructions, Adams left France with his son, returning to America on March 8, 1779, and Massachusetts on August 9, 1779.

In November 1779, Adams set sail again for France, this time as the sole minister for negotiating a trade agreement with Britain after the end of the war. And this time, he was with both sons, John Quincy, age 12, and Charles, age 8.

Three days outside of Boston, his ship was in a storm that lasted for three days, during which time the vessel sprung a leak. The ship's main mast was struck by lightning, destroying it and crippling its ability to move.

All hands were required to pump water for two weeks straight to keep it from sinking.

Initially, they had intended to make port at Bordeaux, France, but their damages drove them to select a slightly closer port at the northwest corner of Spain, at the port city of Ferrol. Instead of waiting a month for the ship's repair, they took the overland route to France on donkeys. Because of this, they had the grueling task of crossing the Pyrenees Mountains in winter. It took them six weeks overland to reach Paris.

To make matters worse, they had to sail through the

British blockade, suffering an attack by the British navy. Cannonballs were whizzing overhead, any one of which could have killed Adams instantly. During the battle, Adams refused to stay below while others were dying to save him, for he was the reason behind their voyage. Recall that John Adams had regretted not fighting in the French and Indian War years earlier.

As a diplomat, Adams suffered from impatience and blunt communication. After several months, the French foreign minister would no longer speak to Adams but only with Franklin.

In mid-1780, Adams first went to the Dutch Republic to seek loans. When that stalled, even after the British defeat at Yorktown, he sought official recognition of the new nation.

On April 19, 1782, the States General of the Netherlands officially recognized the United States of America, and the house in which John Adams lived became the first United States embassy in a foreign country.

THE PHILADELPHIA CAMPAIGN

General William Howe had one plan which seized virtually all of his attention: To take the rebel capital at Philadelphia. He had given only nominal support to General Burgoyne, who was moving down from Canada to divide the rebel colonies, and this was possibly a far more critical strategy. Perhaps he did not believe in Burgoyne's approach, but it had been approved by the government. And besides, ego drove him to be less supportive of a competing officer. Such jealousies are to be expected amongst such aggressive men.

Howe's brother, Vice Admiral Lord Viscount Richard Howe, had arrived at New York with over 200 ships. In preparation for the invasion of the rebel capital, William Howe loaded some 17,000 troops onto his brother's ships starting on July 16, 1777. Nine days later, the fleet of ships left Sandy Hook, New Jersey, which stands across Lower New York Bay from Staten Island.

At first, the ships headed southward along the coast of New Jersey. The plan was to bypass Delaware Bay and River and to head farther south to Chesapeake Bay and then northward to the farthest reaches of the bay to start their inland march toward Philadelphia. The Delaware River would have led directly to Philadelphia, which was likely heavily guarded by rebel ships and cannons.

Going overland from Sandy Hook, the troops likely could have made the trip in a few days. It was only about 67 miles (108 kilometers) away. Their destination by sea was Head of Elk, Maryland (modern Elkton), only 40 miles (65 kilometers) from the rebel capital.

As it was, the trip was far more arduous than either of the Howe brothers had anticipated. Almost immediately, problems slowed them down, including storms, ships colliding with one another, and numerous shortages. A full 28 days at sea left them low on water, food, and fodder. A few of the horses had to be thrown overboard to end their suffering.

Once Howe's men arrived in Maryland on August 25, 1777, they spent another week replenishing their supplies. To the commanders, that was disappointing enough. General Howe had expected a legion of local help from British Loyalists ready to fight the rebels. Still, he found virtually no one willing to join the cause for king and mother country.

During the week of foraging, Howe unloaded the remaining supplies, weapons, horses, and men.

In the meantime, General Washington inserted 11,000 of his men between the British and the capital. However, his men were outflanked at the September 11th Battle of Brandywine, suffering as many as a thousand casualties. Washington was driven back and forced to decide between protecting the capital and protecting his supplies. If he had chosen to protect the capital, it would have been a short-lived success; without his supplies he would have been more easily destroyed by the British. So, he chose to protect his supplies and to lose the capital. And that loss weighed heavily on him.

The Continental Congress moved from Philadelphia to Lancaster and later to York, Pennsylvania.

Contrary to Howe's expectations, his taking of the capital city on September 26 did nothing to end the conflict. This fact went against every tradition of European warfare. Taking a nation's capital had been tantamount to taking the nation's heart, mind, and soul, but not with these Americans. These Americans were most infuriating. Metaphorically, Howe had placed all of his eggs in this one basket, and the results were not what he expected. He had gambled on this potent maneuver and effectively abandoned Burgoyne with support that was too little and too late.

Combined with the news he was sure to receive in short order — that Burgoyne had lost at Saratoga — the war to quell the rebellion was taking some uncomfortable turns.

The British settled into the capital for the winter, establishing garrisons and protecting their supply line along the Delaware River.

Several smaller battles continued into early December, with minor successes on both sides.

Washington had his critics in the American government, and some of them started discussions to have him removed. When the American General heard these secretive discussions, he took his case before the Continental Congress. No more whispers. He wanted the bright light of open examination. Either he would have unanimous and wholehearted support, or he would not be able to do his job. Washington's supporters came to his aid, and Congress reaffirmed his leadership.

TEST YOUR UNDERSTANDING

Answers to the following questions may be found in the Appendix.

1. What gave the Americans the most significant advantage during the Forage War?

•Foragers did not take cannons with them.

•Foragers were in isolated groups far from the protection of their garrisons.

•Foragers needed money in exchange for the goods they sought and frequently did not have enough.

•Foragers were never armed because they had to concentrate on gathering food and supplies.

2. What was the purpose of Burgoyne's Offensive?

•To distract the Americans while General Howe took Philadelphia.

•To reinforce the British hold on New York City.

•To harass the colonial rebels so they would give up.

•To split the colonies along the Hudson River Valley.

3. What was the most significant risk to the British in their occupation of New York City?

•Alienating the citizens and creating more enemies of the crown.

•Running out of provisions as they had in the Siege of Boston.

•Exceeding their budget by paying for room and board throughout their extended stay.

•Running out of wood for the fires required to cook their food and heat their quarters in winter.

4. What contributed to Burgoyne's loss at Saratoga?

•General Barry St. Leger failed to arrive with reinforcements from the West.

•Reinforcements and logistical support never arrived in time from New York City.

•His own Native American warriors abandoned him.

•All of the above.

5. Why did the British not initially treat captured Americans as prisoners of war?

•The King had ordered that the Americans be given no quarter.

•To the British military officers, Americans were merely traitors, not enemy combatants.

•Americans had abused captured British soldiers, and this was retaliation.

•All of the above.

SUMMING IT UP

Ice Age weather played an integral part in the war of the 18th century as it had in centuries past. Armies tended to find shelter to survive the long months of bitter cold. An army without a strong supply line must live off the land and what they can find nearby. Foraging parties became prime targets of the local militia.

The British were anxious to bring the rebellion to a rapid close. Two generals had conflicting ideas about how best to achieve this goal. General Burgoyne wanted to split the northern colonies from the middle and southern colonies to weaken them. Meanwhile, General Howe wanted to capture the rebel capital, confident that this would mean instant victory. Perhaps Burgoyne's campaign was the better plan. Still, General Howe's intended support was too weak and too late to prevent the defeat at Saragota.

Because of the Saratoga victory, European nations who

wanted Great Britain to lose were emboldened to support the American rebels. Benjamin Franklin and his fellow negotiators secured significant support from France, plus additional aid from Spain, the Dutch Republic, and, to a lesser extent, a few other nations, like Denmark, Norway, Portugal, and Russia.

Though John Adams was not a skilled negotiator, he helped to establish official recognition for the young nation by the Dutch Republic, establishing the first U.S. embassy on foreign soil.

Though General Howe's Philadelphia Campaign got off to a rocky start, he was able to complete his mission, yet capturing the rebel capital did not have the decisive effect upon which he had counted.

The Patriots continued their struggle, but now they had the help of the French. Many more challenges and defeats awaited the Americans before they could gain their precious liberty.

WAR GAINS PACE

*T*he war for American independence had been going on for some 30 months when General Washington decided to winter in Valley Forge, Pennsylvania. Emboldened with the aid of the French and, to a lesser degree, that of the Spanish and the Dutch, America's rebel leaders hunkered down for the long, arduous struggle ahead. 1778 to 1779 were in the middle of this conflict, though Washington and the Continental Congress could not have known how long they would have to suffer through the war.

THE WINTER AT VALLEY FORGE

The winter at Valley Forge was undoubtedly uncomfortable for Washington and his men. Still, in a real sense, this was nothing new. All winters for soldiers during an active war are uncomfortable. It is a myth that the suffering at Valley Forge was unusual compared to other winters.

Before winter set in, Washington had his men build log cabins roughly 14 feet by 16 feet. Approximately 1,300 to 1,500 cabins were built, with some estimates going as high as

2,000. These were arranged in orderly rows, made of logs from the abundant nearby forests. So, conditions at Valley Forge were not as dire as the later myths portrayed.

Every winter had supply problems, especially food and clothing. But the men had their shelters built before the coldest weather set in. Also, disease spread more easily amongst the men in such close quarters. By spring, as many as 2,500 of the original 12,000 men had died from disease and malnutrition.

For a short while, Valley Forge qualified as the fourth-largest city in the American colonies. In the context of our modern cities, Valley Forge and even New York were small to medium-sized towns. Today, a small city has over a hundred thousand people, and New York has over 8 million.

Washington chose Valley Forge because it was just a short distance from the British winter encampment in Philadelphia, but not too close for the British to attack easily. Valley Forge was protected on one side by the Schuylkill River and embraced by two hills offering protective high ground.

Some men had their wives and children nearby, which helped them survive the winter. Even Martha Washington stayed awhile, helping deliver supplies to those who needed them most.

Washington trained his men into a precision fighting force during the late autumn, winter, and early spring months. The Continental Army learned their new skills under the tutelage of Prussian-born American General Baron Friedrich Wilhelm von Steuben.

On May 6, 1778, Washington and his men received word of official support from France, news which General Marquis de Lafayette also found welcome since he had arrived well in advance of support becoming a matter of treaty obligation. Celebrations ensued.

THE MARCH FROM PHILADELPHIA

General Howe felt that he had received insufficient support in his war effort and, in October of 1777, sent a letter of resignation to London. Though he had been successful in taking Philadelphia, despite several mishaps getting there, he had been so focused on what he considered to be the "big prize" of the capital city that he ignored his other responsibilities, giving only half-hearted support to Burgoyne in his campaign from Canada. Burgoyne's loss and the fact that the Americans did not surrender once he had captured their capital may have contributed to his resignation.

On May 18, 1778, men loyal to General Howe threw for him a grand party in his honor. Perhaps as a last hurrah, Howe attempted to capture the French General De Lafayette that night but failed.

On May 24, 1778, General Howe sailed for England, leaving General Clinton in command of British forces on the continent.

Upon hearing that the French were now involved with these American rebels, the British under General Clinton feared the French navy would blockade the Delaware River, cutting off their main supply line. Thus, Clinton planned to abandon Philadelphia and return to New York City to consolidate his forces there.

The Loyalists in Philadelphia were alarmed at being left to fend for themselves. They offered to scrape together 3,000 recruits if General Clinton would leave 2,000 of his troops behind to help protect the city from the rebels under Washington. Instead, Clinton recommended that they negotiate peace with the Continental Army if they wanted to stay. Many of them opted to go with the British troops.

Along the way back to New York, the British Red Coats betrayed their cause several times by destroying New Jersey citizens' property and taking food and supplies at will. Even more Americans were now made angry by the abusive British.

New Jersey militia, along with the Continental Army, harassed the British army into exhaustion as they made their way back to the relative safety of the city.

BATTLE OF MONMOUTH, NEW JERSEY

On the morning of June 28, 1778, the competing armies met at Monmouth. American forces, led by General Charles Lee, faced off against the British under General Sir Henry Clinton. The day was scorching in early summer, making the five hours of fighting even more arduous.

General Lee attacked too quickly, which left his forces vulnerable, and he had to retreat until General Washington arrived with the main contingent.

Clinton continued moving his men to New York City in the dark of night.

Lee was later court-martialed for the blunder and for later disrespecting his commander-in-chief.

Though neither side could claim victory at Monmouth, the American troops showed their new skills with valor—skills they had learned during the brutal winter at Valley Forge.

MOLLY PITCHER, ABIGAIL ADAMS, AND OTHER WOMEN REVOLUTIONARIES

Wives and children lived near their husbands at Valley Forge. These "camp followers" continued supporting their husbands throughout the war.

One woman named Deborah Sampson (1760–1827) did not want to be left behind. She disguised herself as a man and served as a soldier in the Continental Army. But fighting on the front line was not the only way women could contribute to the cause of liberty.

MOLLY PITCHER

During the Battle of Monmouth, Molly Pitcher helped the war effort by taking water to the soldiers firing the cannons. When her husband became wounded, she helped by taking over his gun to keep up the assault against the British.

This was not her only act of heroism. She did more than idly sit by through many battles while her husband and other men fought for American liberty.

"Molly Pitcher" is likely a nickname given by the troops to whom she would bring pitchers of water while they fought. Her real name is thought to have been Mary Ludwig Hays McCauley (1754–1832), and she was an inspiration to other women during the war.

ABIGAIL ADAMS

Wife of attorney John Adams, Abigail Adams (1744–1818), supported her husband in his duties to the young nation. When John traveled to Europe to help negotiate for support from France and the Netherlands, she did not complain when he took their sons. Instead, she merely asked him to "Remember the ladies" while helping to create this new nation. The married couple spent many months apart because of his travels, but she bravely took charge of their home in Massachusetts while he was away. Years after the war, her husband was destined to become the second president of these United States, and her son, John Quincy Adams, became the sixth president.

MERCY OTIS WARREN

Massachusetts poet and essayist Mercy Otis Warren (1728–1814) was a friend to Abigail Adams and a strong supporter of American independence. Her passionate and logical essays helped to convince many of her fellow Massachusites to join in the independence effort.

After the war, she published a 3-volume history of the conflict with Great Britain.

PHILLIS WHEATLEY

Before she was ten years old, she was taken from her home in West Africa and sold into slavery. The Wheatley family purchased her in the American colonies, giving her the name Phillis Wheatley (c. 1753–1784). Immediately, they recognized her intelligence and ensured her education. She turned to literature, writing and publishing in 1773, *Poems on Various Subjects, Religious and Moral.* Her work earned praise both in England and in America. The book's 39 poems raised numerous questions about slavery, leading the way with an added dimension to liberty not realized until nearly a century later.

SIBYL LUDINGTON

In the spring of 1777, Sibyl Ludington (1761–1839) was one of many who learned of a British attack in Danbury, Connecticut. Like Paul Revere two years earlier, she rode her horse to warn the militia in surrounding counties to repulse the surprise assault. Unlike Revere's famous ride, Ludington rode through pouring rain at twice the distance, through two counties (Dutchess and Putnam) of the New York former colony.

NANCY HART

Similar to the story of Molly Pitcher, modern historians have very few primary sources from which to confirm the stories regarding Nancy Hart (c. 1735–1830). In the northeast Georgia hinterlands, she was every bit the frontierswoman — a brave and savvy world-builder. Whether or not she was a myth made up to bolster Patriot morale remains uncertain. Still, she is said to have staged numerous attacks against Loyalists, earning her the apt nickname "The Iron Lady." If the stories are true, she outsmarted the British in the art of war and may have shot a few of the Red Coats in the process.

MARGARET CORBIN

Like Molly Pitcher, Margaret Corbin (1751–1800) fought alongside her husband, though her story took place a year and a half earlier, during the British attack on Fort Washington, one of the last strongholds in the New York City area. The fort was situated at the north end of Manhattan Island. After the British overcame the Patriots in November 1776, Margaret was amongst those thought to be dead, next to her husband, who also had manned one of the cannons. Luckily, she was found and treated for her wounds, though they had been severe enough to make her disabled for the remainder of her life. Because of her bravery, she became the first woman to receive an American soldier's pension — a lifetime reward for her service and her husband's sacrifice.

BETSY ROSS

Elizabeth "Betsy" Griscom Ross (1752–1836), an American upholsterer and seamstress, is said to have been the one to make the first American flag with 13 stripes (alternating red and white) and 13 stars, representing the 13 original colonies which became the first states of these United States.

Modern historians point out that the story appears to have originated in the 1870s, about the time of the American Centennial, and was spread by her grandson, William Canby.

The fact that Congress created the legislation known as the Flag Act and passed it in June 1777, half a year after Betsy Ross supposedly made her flag, suggests to some that the story is little more than familial pride and wishful thinking.

Betsy Ross spent the better part of her adult life making flags. Hence, there is some merit to the possibility that the myth is indeed fact, or at least based partly on fact.

Evidence has a nasty habit of disappearing. A lack of a paper trail does not disprove a hypothesis or claim of fact. Traditions handed down in a family may or may not be accurate. The best we can say without corroborating evidence is, "We don't know." What is clear, however, is that Mrs. Ross made countless flags for the young nation and for other purposes, including those for the Pennsylvania Navy.

MARTHA WASHINGTON

The wife of the commander-in-chief, General George Washington, Martha Dandridge Washington (1731–1802), would visit the wintering sites of the Continental Army to help attend to the needs of the soldiers.

Though she initially lived at their home in Mount Vernon, she ended up moving to the home of her brother-in-law so that she would not become an obvious target of the British, who may have wished to kidnap her as leverage against General Washington.

While with her husband during the war, Martha would sew soldiers' uniforms and even instilled in the other wives the desire to help in a similar fashion.

Her husband informed her of the war's progress, including telling her some military secrets. She would also help with clerical work in support of her husband.

As much as any other woman who had helped give birth to this young nation, Martha Washington was a genuine heroine of the Revolutionary War.

WAR ON THE PERIPHERY AND AT SEA

Arguably, the more significant part of the Revolutionary War was held at sea. While the British navy was well-oiled, the American naval forces were scattered, decentralized, and opportunistic. One well-equipped British warship could produce more firepower than the entire Continental Army, and the British had more ships and cannons.

Effectively, the British could blockade the Americans to prevent trade with the rest of the world. Their ships could raid coastal towns at will, creating mayhem up and down the Eastern seaboard. And with their ships, the British could transport troops and supplies where they were most needed.

In 1776, Congress ordered Esek Hopkins to find more gunpowder, which the war effort desperately needed. He was to have his ships capture the town of Nassau in the Bahamas and confiscate whatever supplies they could find. Besides capturing ships there and on the way back, they did manage to acquire even more gunpowder.

Of course, both sides had some stellar failures, like when lousy weather conspired against British General William Howe and his brother Admiral Richard Howe in transporting troops from New York to the upper Chesapeake Bay during the Philadelphia Campaign. What should have taken days turned into arduous weeks.

At the start of the conflict in 1775, the Americans were outclassed on land and sea. The colonial rebels may have lost if it had not been for the French entry into the American cause for liberty with its powerful French navy. The British, after all, had the most powerful navy in the world.

Maintaining a navy was expensive, and Congress needed more funds. To make up for this, the American Patriot leaders employed a technique used by the Romans some two millennia earlier — allowing those who fought in the wars to take booty from their successes. To this end, Congress depended heavily on these privateers to slow down the British. While ground forces directly under General Washington rarely exceeded 10,000, the crews of privateer ships numbered approximately 55,000 sailors. Throughout the war, roughly 1,700 American ships took 2,283 British ships. This not only proved costly to the enemy but enriched the privateers and their crews from the otherwise illicit sale of stolen cargo and the sale of each ship.

After the start of 1778, the Americans had support from the French navy under Vice-Admiral Comte Charles Henri Hector d'Estaing and Vice-Admiral François Joseph Paul de Grasse, the Spanish naval forces under Admiral Luis de Córdova y Córdova, and the Dutch Republic ships under Rear Admiral Johan Zoutman.

Although the British navy was more powerful, the French navy came in at a strong second. When Vice-Admiral d'Estaing sailed to the Americas, the British did not immediately send more ships after him because they did not want to leave their homeland vulnerable. And unlike the Seven Years' War two decades earlier, the British could not count on a counterforce to distract the French. The other European nations were busy with their concerns or were fighting with the French and the Americans against the British.

Because Great Britain and France were at war, the conflict was not confined to the Americas. Still, it remained a global concern because of the worldwide placement of

British, French, Spanish, and Dutch territories. At least 1,200 warships were involved, including 25,000 naval cannons and more than a quarter million sailors. These numbers made the land battles of 10,000 and 12,000 men with a few dozen cannons seem insignificant by comparison.

American bravery and hit-and-run tactics kept their Continental Navy and state navies from being destroyed. After the French, Spanish, and Dutch navies entered the conflict, American naval ships were relegated mainly to privateering — capturing British merchant ships and taking them to French or Spanish ports.

In 1778, 12 French ships under Vice-Admiral d'Estaing were ordered to the Delaware Bay to blockade supplies, sent up the Delaware River to General Howe, and, later, to his replacement, General Clinton, in Philadelphia. By the time the French ships had arrived, the British had already abandoned Philadelphia.

Vice-Admiral d'Estaing turned his ships northward to New York but found the sandbars impossible to cross then and decided to attack Newport, Rhode Island. American forces landed and began preparing for a siege. At the same time, British Admiral Howe arrived with a smaller contingent of ships to attack the French. Again, the weather quickly soured, turning into a raging storm for two days, damaging many of the vessels. When the weather cleared, there were several skirmishes. Still, d'Estaing's flagship was damaged, and he returned to the Americans outside of Newport to tell them he could not assist in their attack. Instead, he headed for Boston to begin repairs. The Americans were furious.

In September 1778, Admiral John Byron replaced Admiral Howe and continued the pursuit of the French forces. Another storm scattered Byron's fleet while attempting to blockade d'Estaing at Boston, but the French fleet slipped away and headed for the West Indies.

Also, in 1778, the British captured Savannah, Georgia, and a year later, French and American forces attempted to recapture the city but failed. Many of the French ships were sufficiently damaged that they sailed home to France for repairs.

Late in 1781, the French fleet proved crucial in preventing British General Cornwallis from receiving reinforcements or supplies, leading to his surrender and the war's end.

HARSH WINTER; DEADLOCK IN NEW YORK, THE OHIO RIVER VALLEY, AND THE SIEGE OF SAVANNAH

The winter of 1779–1780 played its role nearly two years before the British surrender at Yorktown. Though Washington's men suffered greatly in prior winters, this was the worst. They had endured the cold of 1776–1777, crossing the ice-clogged Delaware River. They carried on despite the hardships of Valley Forge in the winter of 1777–1778. But with 28 snowstorms, several feet of snow, and temperatures almost always below freezing, wildlife virtually disappeared. Provisions for 10,000 troops became scarce. It is said that men would roast their shoes. Ink froze in the quills of the officers. Each saltwater inlet was choked with ice from Canada down to North Carolina. In New York harbor, the ice was sufficiently thick for British soldiers to march from the city to Staten Island, even dragging artillery over the frozen waters. After the winter, George Washington wrote, "The oldest people now living in this Country do not remember so hard a winter as the one we are now emerging from. In a word, the severity of the frost exceeded anything of the kind that had ever been experienced in this climate before."

The conflicts of the Revolutionary War spilled out across the larger American landscape, with battles, skirmishes, and sieges taking place far from General Washington and the core of his Continental Army. Consider three regions during 1779 and in the larger context of the war: New York, the Ohio River Valley, and Savannah.

NEW YORK IN CONTEXT

After Washington was forced to abandon New York City in 1776, the British held the city until after the war. Throughout the war, New York City became the British command center and base of operations.

By early 1779, General Washington had deployed parts of his Continental Army in locations around the city with orders to avoid being drawn out by British tactics. British General Clinton wanted desperately to engage directly with Washington and sought to provoke him by attacking his supply lines. In late May 1779, sailing up the Hudson River from New York City, Clinton deployed an 8,000-man force to take Stony Point from a small contingent of Americans. Clinton left 750 men at Stony Point and had the fortifications built there protected on the river by several ships.

But this was uncomfortably close to Washington's chief stronghold on the Hudson River at West Point, several miles upriver from Stony Point.

Washington assigned to General "Mad Anthony" Wayne the retaking of Stony Point and, in mid-July, Wayne's forces of about 1,500 men marched into position, taking into custody any civilians they encountered to prevent them from warning the British. The plan was for Wayne's forces to attack at night, so they pinned small bits of very visible white paper to their hats so they could more easily distinguish his men from the British.

On the evening of July 15, Wayne was aided by bad weather. Clouds covered the Moon, and high winds forced the British ships guarding Stony Point to move southward to calmer waters.

From midnight to 1:00 a.m. on July 16, 1779, General Wayne's forces rushed up the hill to capture the British position. So rapid was the stealthy advancement that the British were unable to lower their cannons in time to thwart the attack. Some of Wayne's Patriots had already passed the first line of defense before the alarm sounded. The British under Colonel Henry Johnson were taken prisoner and, to their surprise, were shown uncommon decency despite the cruelty the British had shown to Americans captured in earlier battles.

The success at Stony Point did much to boost American morale, but because it lacked strategic importance, Washington had it abandoned two days later. And though the British retook Stony Point, they abandoned it three months later.

There is no doubt that Washington wanted to retake New York City. Still, with his far more limited resources, he had to settle for a relative stalemate.

And though the British continued to hold out in New York, they had other problems with which to contend. A little over a month after the scuffle at Stony Point, British Captain John Peebles noticed that soldiers were getting sick in increasing numbers.

"The number of sick increasing every day, in all the different Camps of the army," he wrote on September 5, 1779. A week later, he wrote, "The Men growing very sickly within these few days, a general complaint over the whole army, they are mostly taken with headache & universal pain a chill & feverishness, which for the most part turns into a quotidian or tertian intermittent, & some few are rather with the flux."

Though only 12 out of 100 of his men fell ill, with three fatalities, other companies were not so lucky, suffering a greater number of deaths. Though Peebles remarked that the summer had been rainy, with little wind and no lightning, the ultimate cause may have been the ships received in August carrying new troops from England. Several hundred had been ill, with several deaths while crossing the Atlantic.

OHIO RIVER VALLEY IN CONTEXT

For the far western regions of the former American colonies, the Revolutionary War was merely a blurred continuation of the intermittent wars the frontier settlers had suffered ever since their arrival. For some, the French and Indian War never really ended. At least, the Native Americans never got the memo that hostilities had ceased.

The Ohio River Valley had been declared off-limits by King George III in 1763 after the regional French and Indian War and the larger Seven Years' War had been completed. But settlers had already moved into that territory and were not about to give up what they had built. The crown, however, did not want to suffer the extra expense of sending their military into that wilderness to occupy and protect.

BATTLE OF POINT PLEASANT

Despite this, the Americans negotiated in 1768 with the Iroquois to acquire lands west of Virginia and south of the Ohio River — currently West Virginia and Kentucky. This would have been sufficient if the Iroquois had been the only other interested parties, but a number of different tribes objected, most notably the Shawnee and Mingo. Under the governor of the colony, Lord Dunmore, Virginians had negotiated with many of the neighboring tribes to create division between them and the Shawnee.

In the only combat — Battle of Point Pleasant, also known as the Battle of Kanawha — of what became known as Dunmore's War, October 10, 1774, the Virginians were victorious, ultimately forcing the Shawnee to relinquish any claims they had to lands south and east of the Ohio Valley. As the last Virginian forces returned home in early 1775, hostilities broke out in Massachusetts, initiating the Revolutionary War.

Of historical note, one of the men killed in that western battle was Colonel John Field, two descendants of whom became presidents of these United States—George H. W. Bush and his son, George W. Bush.

The Battle of Point Pleasant was a precursor of what the Americans would suffer at the hands of Native American tribes, who were later encouraged with supplies and promises by the British to attack the settlers. The chief British source of trouble for the western settlers was General Hamilton, stationed at Fort Detroit.

BATTLES AT FORT HENRY AND THE FOREMAN MASSACRE

At what is today Wheeling, West Virginia, stood Fort Henry on the western frontier of the former colonies. In August 1777, Native Americans attacked the fort resulting in calls for militia support. One of those who answered the call was Captain William Foreman. Late the following month, citizens noticed smoke rising toward the south. They grew concerned that the settlement at McMechen was under attack. Colonel David Shepherd, commander at Fort Henry, sent Captain Foreman and 43 men to investigate. Finding everyone safe at McMechen, Foreman and his men stayed the night and returned northward the following morning, September 27, 1777.

Captain Lynn was worried that taking the same return path might prove dangerous in case a native scout saw them the previous day. Lynn suggested taking the ridge route back to the fort. Foreman rejected the suggestion, but Lynn took the ridge route. On the way back, Foreman and 20 of his men were ambushed by roughly two dozen Native Americans. Lynn and his men heard the shots fired and came down the hill, making as much noise as possible, scaring off the Native Americans. Most of the men with Foreman were killed, including his two sons.

Numerous other Native American raids were made against settlements in the Greenbrier and Monongahela regions, killing soldiers and civilians alike.

The last battle of the Revolutionary War took place at Fort Henry, Virginia (Wheeling, West Virginia), September 11–13, 1782. Americans loyal to the crown, and many Native Americans attacked the fort. During the fighting, the commander, Colonel Shepherd, remarked they were getting dangerously low on gunpowder. Betty Zane, 17 years old, volunteered to retrieve some from her brother's house several dozen yards from the fort. Her heroism allowed the American Patriots to hold off the attackers.

SIEGE OF FORT LAURENS

About 50 miles due west of the triple junction of current state borders of Ohio, West Virginia, and Pennsylvania, at the point where the Ohio River leaves Pennsylvania, stood Fort Laurens. It was built in December 1778 and named after a president of the Continental Congress, Henry Laurens of South Carolina. One purpose for the fort was to act as a staging area for a planned attack on the British at Detroit.

The winter of 1778–1779 proved sufficiently harsh that the commander moved most of his men to eastern Pennsylvania's Fort Pitt. Only about 150 soldiers were left at Fort Laurens. On February 22, 1779, British Captain Henry Bird laid siege on the fort with his men and some 200 native warriors of the Delaware, Mingo, Munsee, and Wyandot tribes. The siege lasted for roughly four weeks, after which both sides were significantly weakened from the lack of food. On March 23, 1779, three days after the British withdrawal, American soldiers from Fort Pitt came to relieve those who had held out during the winter months.

A new commander at Fort Pitt, Colonel Daniel Brodhead, reassessed the suitability of Fort Laurens for staging an assault on Fort Detroit and found it lacking. On August 2, 1779, he had Fort Laurens abandoned.

SAVANNAH, GEORGIA, IN CONTEXT

British forces took Savannah, Georgia, in December 1778 as part of their "Southern Strategy." They had hoped to gain the support of Loyalists in the South but found the estimates of their numbers to be overly exaggerated. However, British promises of freedom to slaves generated a large number of recruits to make up for the lack of Loyalist support. Savannah had been their first target. Later, they would attempt to take Charleston, South Carolina.

By modern standards, colonial cities were no more than towns. Savannah had fewer than 5,000 people and did not rank in the top ten cities of the Americas by population. Even so, Savannah was the major seaport for the entire Georgia territory. By comparison, Charleston had about 16,000 civilians.

On September 3, 1779, American General Benjamin Lincoln learned that French Admiral Comte d'Estaing would soon arrive at Savannah with his fleet of ships and an army of roughly 4,000 soldiers.

Eight days later, Lincoln left Charleston with about 2,000 men, headed for Savannah, leaving behind roughly 4,000 soldiers to defend the region around the city.

The following day, September 12, the French admiral's fleet started to arrive and began disembarking troops. On September 16, the French started to move on the city.

The British occupying force under General Augustine Prévost numbered about 2,000, nearly half the size of the civilian population. But the British general had ordered Colonel John Maitland to return to Savannah with about 1,000 troops stationed elsewhere.

Because of the overwhelming French presence, the admiral gave General Prévost the option of surrender, but the British general asked for a 24-hour truce while he considered the offer, and Admiral Comte d'Estaing agreed.

General Lincoln was supposed to prevent Maitland's men from reinforcing those at Savannah, but a mix-up in communications resulted in an opening through which Maitland was able to reach the city before the French truce ended. General Prévost politely rejected the suggestion that he surrender.

When the American general arrived at Savannah, the combined ground forces against the British numbered about 5,000. And while the French had arrived with 42 ships, the British had only 8.

Between September 19 and October 16, 1779, the Americans and French laid siege on Savannah in an attempt to reclaim the city.

From the start, the assault went badly. A squadron of French ships engaged with three British ships, but the following day, the British scuttled one ship leaking badly. And they did this at a narrow section of the channel, effectively blocking the French from getting closer to the city to support the American assault.

Against advice to attack British defenses, d'Estaing decided to bombard the city with cannon fire, so he offloaded several guns and shelled the city from October 3 through 8. The horrible damage he caused did not have the effect he had expected. In addition, the French admiral was becoming increasingly impatient to finish with Savannah because many of his men suffered from scurvy and dysentery.

A surprise attack scheduled for the morning of October 9 went awry partly because troops sent to attack one of the British redoubts got lost in the morning fog. Scottish sharpshooters found it easy to pick off the French soldiers in their bright, white uniforms at another British redoubt.

American and French losses mounted steadily, and d'Estaing ordered a retreat.

Lincoln and d'Estaing studied their options and decided that the British were too secure. On October 17, they abandoned the siege of Savannah.

TEST YOUR UNDERSTANDING

Answers to the following questions may be found in the Appendix.

1. What did George Washington and his men accomplish at Valley Forge?

•Roughly 80% of his men survived the cold, malnutrition, and disease to continue fighting in 1778.

•They built what amounted to the fourth largest city in the 13 states in a matter of weeks.

•The soldiers trained into a precision fighting force.

•All of the above.

2. What good news did Washington and his men receive at Valley Forge?

•That the Marquis de Lafayette would be arriving from France with food and clothing.

•That the French had forced the British to leave America's capital city of Philadelphia.

•That Margaret Corbin would receive a soldier's pension for her courageous sacrifice at the battle to defend Fort Washington.

•That the French government would openly support the American cause for liberty.

3. Why did British General Clinton abandon Philadelphia?

•He feared the French ships would cut off his supply lines by blockading the Delaware River.

•Washington's army was leaving Valley Forge and heading straight for his men guarding the city.

•Because his predecessor, General Howe, had failed to capture General Marquis de Lafayette.

•Because the harsh winter cold had left his men too weak to fight against Washington's growing army of Patriots.

4. Which woman helped fight the British retreating from Philadelphia by manning the cannon after her husband was wounded?

•Mercy Otis Warren.

•Molly Pitcher.

•Sibyl Ludington.

•Betsy Ross.

5. What mistakes during the Siege of Savannah led to the failure of Americans to reclaim the city?

•Admiral d'Estaing's cannon kept missing their targets in Savannah.

•The French scuttled one of their damaged ships at a

narrow part of the channel but then realized that they had blocked closer access of their remaining ships to the city.

•General Lincoln's men failed to stop Maitland's reinforcements from reaching Savannah.

•All of the above.

SUMMING IT UP

Though General Washington suffered significant losses from disease and malnutrition from his army's wintering at Valley Forge, the majority who survived ended up being a more formidable fighting force from the training they had received from General von Steuben.

With General Howe's resignation, General Clinton took charge of the British army fighting the Americans. Upon hearing that the French had entered the war, he had Philadelphia abandoned because of the vulnerability of his supply line on the Delaware River. Many Loyalists left the city with Clinton and his men.

Many women performed acts of heroism not only in support of their Patriot husbands or friends but also by their direct action, either through writing or through taking up arms against the British. The most famous were Molly Pitcher, Abigail Adams, and Martha Washington.

A far greater number of men and cannons were employed in the battles at sea than were committed to those on land. Ships allowed one side or the other to transport troops relatively quickly, blockade ports, and acquire needed resources, like the mission undertaken by American Commodore Esek Hopkins to obtain much-needed gunpowder for the war.

British took Stony Point from the Americans, which was too close to chief defensive position on the Hudson River at West Point. But a daring midnight raid by General Anthony Wayne recaptured the small defensive position.

Numerous battles took place throughout the Revolutionary War in the Ohio River Valley. One combination or another of British troops, Loyalists, and Native Americans attacked the Americans making life in the continental wilderness continually dangerous.

The Americans and French attempted to reclaim Savannah, but a series of mistakes led to failure, with the British maintaining their hold on Georgia's main port city.

Great Britain's Southern Strategy continued after the taking of Savannah in late 1778 and holding off the American attempt to retake the city in 1779. Next on their list was Charles Town, South Carolina.

REBELLION REVERBERATES

*T*he year 1780 was marked by several failures and a major betrayal by a trusted officer.

SIEGE OF CHARLESTON

After the British capture of Savannah, Georgia, in December 1778, the next stage of their Southern Strategy was to capture Charles Town (modern Charleston), South Carolina.

After General Benjamin Lincoln failed to reclaim Savannah in September 1779, American forces fell back to Charleston.

British had some 17,000 troops and sailors, six ships of the line, eight frigates, four armed galleys, and 90 transports. The Americans had only about 6,500 troops and sailors, three frigates, five sloops, one schooner, one brig, and three armed galleys.

General Clinton laid siege after cutting off the supply line into the city.

The Americans were outnumbered and outgunned, and

with lines for resupply and reinforcements cut off, the prospects for holding out did not look good.

With the battle going badly for the Americans, Lincoln attempted for several days to negotiate a surrender with the honors of war, but Clinton refused those and sought unconditional surrender. This could be seen as a mistake on Clinton's part. After Washington learned of this, he vowed to return the favor to the British.

The fall of Charles Town was Lincoln's most significant defeat. The British captured

- 5,266 prisoners,
- 311 pieces of artillery,
- 9,178 artillery rounds,
- 5,916 muskets,
- 33,000 rounds of ammunition, and
- 49 ships.

Though the British had hoped for Loyalists to come to their aid, very few were to be found in the South. The countryside descended into guerrilla warfare, making for an uneasy and somewhat Pyrrhic victory.

THE BATTLE OF CAMDEN

On August 16, 1780, the Americans suffered another loss in Camden, South Carolina.

On June 5, General Clinton returned to New York, leaving it to General Cornwallis to clean up the details in the South. General Washington sent several regiments to the South to help aid the remaining Patriot resistance in the region. He also sent the hero of Saratoga, General Horatio Gates.

Gates ignored important advice from his officers and did not heed their warnings. After his glorious win over Burgoyne at Saratoga, he seemed to become too cocky and not sufficiently cautious. Too, he had been trained in the European method of battle and did not have the skills with Washington's more unpredictable, Fabian, guerrilla-style tactics of wearing out an opponent by delay and evasion rather than confrontation.

While Burgoyne had been relatively weak on strategy, this new opponent Cornwallis was a master of strategy.

The Americans had 1,500 regulars and 2,500 militia, plus eight big guns. The British also had 1,500 regulars but only 600 militia and four guns.

The smaller British force slaughtered the Americans. Of the American forces, 900 were killed or wounded, and the British captured 1,000 men, all eight guns, and more than 200 wagons. Of the British, only 58 were killed and 245 wounded.

BETRAYAL AT WEST POINT

Benedict Arnold was a complex man full of strength but plagued with insecurities. He served with distinction during the first five years of the Revolutionary War. He was responsible, along with Ethan Allen, for capturing Fort Ticonderoga from the British and making it possible for Colonel Henry Knox to acquire for the Americans several dozen tons of armaments that had been transported to Boston to lay siege against the British. Throughout many conflicts, Arnold was wounded in action three times at the battles of Quebec, Ridgefield, and Saratoga.

Arnold had been born into a prestigious New England family. However, his father had been a drunkard, leading the young American to become overly sensitive to any slight against his character. At the start of the war, he was an enthusiastic supporter, quickly rising in the ranks. But his military exploits came with several heavy burdens. While he was on his Ticonderoga Campaign, his first wife died. Later, when his left leg was severely injured during the Battle of Saratoga, he had it crudely set rather than amputated. As a result, his left leg was two inches shorter than his right.

When the British abandoned Philadelphia in 1778, General Washington left Benedict Arnold in charge of the city. Historians have criticized Washington for this choice because Arnold was not the most diplomatic man for such an important job, especially after the city had suffered an extensive occupation by the British.

Benedict Arnold, 37, met 18-year-old Peggy Shippen that summer and courted her. Peggy's father was a Loyalist, and British Major John André had previously courted Peggy during the British occupation of America's capital city. Peggy's father, Judge Edward Shippen, was quite demanding concerning who he would allow to marry his daughter. To prove his worth, Arnold took out a sizable loan to purchase an expensive mansion, but to make payments on the mansion, Arnold and his new wife could not take possession, but instead had to rent out the place to make ends meet.

In dire need of funds and quite possibly at the urging of his young wife, Arnold sent word to British General Clinton that his services were available. And by that time, Major André, young Peggy's former suitor, had become the British spy chief for the ongoing conflict.

When General Anthony Wayne was capturing Stony Point (July 16, 1779), several miles downriver from West Point, Benedict Arnold was already providing British spies with critical information about locations of supply depots and troops, plus the strengths of forces at each location. British General Clinton wanted intelligence on the defenses at West Point and other sites along the Hudson River. Like General Burgoyne, Clinton wanted to cut off the North from the Middle and Southern colonies.

Because Benedict Arnold desperately needed money, he negotiated with the British for compensation, but by October 1779, his discussions with the British command had stalled. In the meantime, Patriots in Philadelphia wanted to rout out all Loyalists, and Arnold and his in-laws were being harassed. To make matters worse, Congress refused to help protect Arnold and his extended family.

In early 1780, Congress held an inquiry into Benedict Arnold's expenses during the Quebec Invasion, but Arnold claimed that the documentation had been lost in the hasty retreat. Congress charged Arnold for the sum of £1,000 because of the missing funds. In early April, Arnold learned from Philip Schuyler that receiving the command at West Point might be possible. By late April, Arnold had resigned from his command at Philadelphia.

By early June 1780, Schuyler had not convinced Washington to give West Point to Benedict Arnold. Still, Arnold sought to reignite the British interests by letting them know of Schuyler's actions, including the man's evaluation of West Point's conditions.

While on his way home to Connecticut, Arnold visited West Point on June 16 and subsequently sent a thorough assessment of the American fort. While in Connecticut, he set in motion the liquidation of all assets, including his family home, and started transferring funds to London through associates in New York City.

In the meantime, André returned to New York on June 18 after serving in the victorious capture of Charleston, South Carolina.

Upon returning to Philadelphia, Arnold sent a more reassuring message on July 7 to British General Clinton, implying that his appointment to the command at West Point was guaranteed. He even discussed a "drawing of the works . . . by which you might take [the fort] without loss."

Becoming impatient, Arnold sent a series of letters before Clinton could respond to his July 7 message. His July 11 message threatened to end negotiations if no progress was immediately forthcoming. His July 12 letter reiterated his intention to surrender West Point, but now his price had become £20,000 with a down payment of £1,000 to be included with their response.

Benedict Arnold obtained his command at West Point on August 3, 1780. Then, on August 15, André delivered Clinton's agreement to the £20,000. Coded messages of treason were difficult to deliver. Still, Arnold continued to tell the British about Washington's movements and plans, plus details about the French. Finally, on August 25, his wife, Peggy, delivered Arnold Clinton's full agreement to his terms.

As commander at West Point, Benedict Arnold held great authority over the entire Hudson River Valley, from Albany to the British lines just north of New York City. From his first day on the job, he began systematically to weaken West Point's defenses and its military strength.

Arnold's acceptance of Clinton's terms was sent on August 30 and included a recommendation that he meet with André. Through a series of mishaps, that meeting did not occur until September 21. On September 22, Arnold gave André a pass to make it through the military lines on his way back to New York. With that pass, Arnold gave André the West Point plans.

Saturday, September 23, 1780, three Westchester militiamen captured André and discovered the papers which exposed the West Point treason. They then turned the British spy over to Colonel John Jameson, and André convinced the officer to return him to General Benedict Arnold at West Point.

When Major Benjamin Tallmadge, a member of General

Washington's network of spies, heard of the apprehension, he insisted that Colonel Jameson return André immediately. What Colonel Jameson did next proved pivotal in the fate of Benedict Arnold.

When the lieutenant escorting André to Arnold had returned with the prisoner, Jameson sent the lieutenant to Benedict Arnold to inform him of André's capture.

On September 24, 1780, General Benedict Arnold received the message that André had been captured. That was bad enough, but he also learned that the papers André had been carrying were sent to General Washington, with whom Arnold was to have breakfast shortly. Instead, Arnold had a barge take him downriver to the HMS *Vulture* and used it to flee to New York City.

Washington negotiated for a prisoner exchange — André for Arnold —but Clinton declined the offer. André was hanged as a spy, and Arnold became a General in the British army fighting against the American Patriots.

GUERRILLA WAR IN SOUTH CAROLINA

The Swamp Fox and father of guerrilla warfare in America, Francis Marion (c. 1732–1795), was born and raised in South Carolina. After the British violence at Lexington and Concord, Marion supported the American call for liberty. He joined on June 21, 1775, as a captain in the 2nd South Carolina Regiment of the Continental Army. Congress commissioned him as a lieutenant colonel in September of the following year. Three years later, in 1779, he was one of the many officers who participated in the failed attempt to reclaim Savannah.

During the Siege of Charles Town, Marion was outside the city recuperating from a broken ankle, so he escaped capture when the city fell. Later, he joined General Gates in time for the Battle at Camden. Because Gates thought poorly of Marion, he sent the junior officer to gather intelligence. Thus Marion missed participating in the battle lost by his fellow Americans.

Because the British effectively subdued the South, Marion could no longer depend on supplies or orders from Washington or Congress. But Marion's Men were different from the regular army. They served the cause without pay, used their own horses and weapons, and often supplied their own food.

Marion's hit-and-run tactics served two purposes — avoiding capture and inflicting maximum damage with minimum risk. Throughout his campaigns to terrorize the British regulars and their Loyalist supporters, he and his men staged their operations from Snow's Island, Florence County.

In one of his first operations, Marion and his men attacked a British encampment from behind and rescued 150 prisoners.

Almost always outnumbered, they operated by stealth. And, because the British never knew where they were, the Red Coats ended up spreading their forces out to cover more territory than would otherwise be required. Marion grew to despise the British even more when they started hanging prisoners instead of holding them. Francis Marion threatened the British that if they did not stop such behavior, he would be obliged to do likewise to any British officers he might catch.

In one encounter, British Lieutenant Colonel Banastre Tarleton chased Marion for seven long hours, covering 26 miles, ultimately losing the Americans in the South Carolina swamps. Tarleton ended up remarking, "As for this damned old fox, the Devil himself could not catch him." And from then on, the Patriot Americans of the South cheered on their

"Swamp Fox."

Because of his many successes in harassing the British, South Carolina's Patriot governor, John Rutledge, commissioned Francis Marion as a brigadier general.

THE BATTLE OF KINGS MOUNTAIN

In the forest and hills of north-central South Carolina, on the border with North Carolina, Patriot resistance continued despite the British wins at Savannah and Charles Town (modern Charleston). The British command desperately wanted to quell the perpetual uprisings. While the Battle of Saratoga was one kind of turning point — a military win that proved to the nations of Europe that the Americans had a serious chance at winning the war, the Battle of Kings Mountain proved to both the British and the Americans that the freedom-loving Patriots were not going to go quietly into defeat. Indeed, the American Patriot win at Kings Mountain showed that even the rough, backcountry militia could overcome a larger Loyalist force.

Only Major Patrick Ferguson was British among the Loyalist forces at Kings Mountain. His men were Loyalist Americans who had hired on to stop the Patriots. And some of those Loyalists had previously fought the British as Patriots, later switching sides.

British General Cornwallis gave Ferguson the task of scraping together a force of Loyalist militia to protect the left flank of Lord Cornwallis at Charlotte, North Carolina, a short distance to the east of Kings Mountain.

After the American losses at Charles Town (May 12, 1780) and Camden (August 16, 1780), a number of American militia collaborated on an offensive against the British in South Carolina, seeing that Generals Lincoln and Gates had left a gaping hole in the Patriot command structure of the South.

By September 25, 1780, several American militia leaders had met at Sycamore Shoals in modern Tennessee.

The following day, British General Cornwallis marched into Charlotte, North Carolina, fully expecting cheers from crowds of Loyalists. To his dismay, he found 150 Patriots. Though the rebel Patriots were quickly dispersed, Cornwallis discovered that occupying Charlotte would become more of a nightmare than he could have imagined.

After Cornwallis took Charlotte, several Patriot militias set out to chase Ferguson and his Loyalists before they could join up with Cornwallis. By October 4, the Patriots had reached Ferguson's old camp at Gilbert Town. And on October 6, the Patriot leaders received word that Ferguson was currently camped at Kings Mountain.

Converging on Major Ferguson's position were the small to medium-sized militias of Colonel William Campbell, Colonel Elijah Clarke, Colonel Benjamin Cleveland, Colonel James Johnston, Major Joseph McDowell, Colonel John Sevier, Colonel Isaac Shelby, and Colonel James Williams.

Mid-afternoon on October 7, several detachments of Patriot militia stormed up the western ridge's steep slope, taking Ferguson and his men by surprise. For an hour, the Patriots alternated between attacks and retreats as the Loyalists chased with bayonets before retreating up the hill to their camp. With 900 Patriots against 1,121 British-led Loyalists, the day's surprise was that the British forces were getting slaughtered.

Colonels Campbell, Sevier, and Shelby had taken their forces to the other side and finally attacked Ferguson from the rear, forcing his men back to their camp. Many white flags appeared, but Ferguson would not have surrendered. The British officer tried to rally his men but was shot by a volley of fire from the Patriots and subsequently dragged by his horse past the Patriot line. One soldier demanded Ferguson surrender, at which point the officer shot the soldier and immediately received seven answering shots from surrounding Patriot militia.

Ferguson's second in command tried to surrender. A large number of Loyalists were killed trying to surrender. With the second attempt to surrender, some patriot officers ran forward to stop the shooting and allow the Loyalists to give up their arms peacefully. However, the Patriot soldiers were still angry at the British slaughtering of Patriots who had tried to surrender in recent battles.

When done, the Patriots had suffered 28 killed and 62 wounded, while the British Loyalists had suffered 290 killed, 163 wounded, and 668 captured.

After 16 days in Charlotte, General Cornwallis left with his men, declaring, "Let's get out of here; this place is a damned hornet's nest." And to this day, Charlotte's official seal includes the image of a hornet's nest.

TEST YOUR UNDERSTANDING

Answers to the following questions may be found in the Appendix.

1. What did American General Lincoln ask of the British before surrendering?

• Not to burn the city to the ground.

• To give Patriot women and children free passage to Patriot-held territory.

• To allow his soldiers to remain free on their honor, not to fight for the remainder of the war.

• To allow the Americans to surrender with the honors of war.

2. what was American General Gates's chief mistake

during the Battle of Camden?

•After his win at Saratoga, thinking that he was invincible.

•Not listening to the advice of his officers.

•Remaining certain that his larger force and greater number of guns would guarantee victory.

•Waiting too long to engage with the enemy.

3. What was the likely cause of Benedict Arnold's betrayal in selling secrets to the enemy?

•His second wife and her family were Loyalists.

•Arnold had racked up a huge debt and needed to raise considerable money.

•He lost faith in the American cause for liberty.

•All of the above.

4. How did Francis Marion get his nickname, the "Swamp Fox?"

•He had a long nose and fox-like eyes.

•After chasing Marion for hours, losing him in the swamp, Lieutenant Colonel Tarleton called him a "fox."

•His detachment of militiamen was the Fox Brigade, and there are many swamps in South Carolina.

•Marion had once become lost in the swamp and was rescued by a fox.

5. What made the Battle of Kings Mountain unique?

•The Americans won.

•The soldiers on both sides were entirely militiamen.

•The British commander abandoned his men when he saw they were losing.

•General Washington arrived just in time to save the Patriots from slaughter.

SUMMING IT UP

The second phase of the British "Southern Strategy" involved taking Charleston, South Carolina, north of their first big win at Savannah, Georgia. The fall of Charleston to the British was a significant loss for the Americans, including the loss of a seasoned officer in General Lincoln, more than 5,000 soldiers, more than 300 pieces of artillery, thousands of rounds of ammunition, and 49 ships.

The Battle of Camden also proved to be a significant loss for the Americans, with the hero of Saratoga ignoring sound advice from his junior officers.

One of the lowest points in the Revolutionary War was the betrayal of General Benedict Arnold, selling secrets to the enemy and plotting to give up the strategic West Point on the Hudson River.

And perhaps it is just as well that General Gates did not respect his junior officers, sending Lt. Colonel Francis Marion on some minor errand, saving the future "Swamp Fox" from capture. Months later, Marion became a central hero to the South by harassing the British with stunning raids with near impunity.

American Patriots could still bleed. They could still lose.

There was no guarantee to have the French, Spanish, and Dutch aid.

But the British found their successes were less solid than they had hoped. The American rascals proved to be hornets and foxes, bedeviling the proper British sensibilities about how war should be conducted.

The expectations of the British were starting to unravel as their Southern Strategy continued to be met with mounting losses and occasional victories achieved at a high cost.

DAWN IS COMING

The tides of war seemed to be turning to favor the Americans, but even close to victory, caution is always recommended. Even though General Cornwallis surrendered at Yorktown, Virginia, the war would not officially be over for another two years. And a lot can happen in two years! Though 1781 proved to be a year filled with great success for the Patriots, other battles would continue to mar the countryside while peace was being negotiated.

THE BATTLE OF COWPENS

Americans continued to resist British order, and Cornwallis was desperate to stop the constant state of rebellion. British and American forces clashed at Cowpens, South Carolina, several miles west of Kings Mountain, nearly six years after the start of the war on January 17, 1781. The battle took place on a field for pasturing cows at the Broad and Pacolet Rivers. After the disastrous loss by General Gates at Camden, South Carolina, General Washington selected General Nathanael Greene to replace him.

On December 3, 1780, less than two months after the brilliant Patriot success at Kings Mountain, Brigadier General Daniel Morgan, under orders from General Washington, reported to General Greene. And Greene, realizing that his small force of fewer than 2,000 men would be no match for the British in a face-to-face battle, decided to split his forces, giving 600 men to Morgan to support Patriots west of the Catawba River and to find supplies that remained too scarce in and around Greene's headquarters at Charlotte. By the end of the year, Morgan's forces had swelled, according to some estimates, to roughly 1,900 men with militiamen from Georgia and throughout the Carolinas. However, Morgan reported to General Greene that his men numbered only 800.

British General Cornwallis got wind of Morgan's movements and, through poor intelligence, thought that the rebel force was headed to take over the fort at Ninety Six, South Carolina. On January 2, 1781, Cornwallis sent Lieutenant Colonel Banastre Tarleton to stop Morgan and to help defend the Loyalist fort. However, when Tarleton reached the fort, Morgan was nowhere to be found. The British officer asked Cornwallis for reinforcements and soon received them, then set out to find Morgan. On January 12, Tarleton received solid intelligence of the rebel leader's location.

Morgan and his men reached the Broad River on January 16. Because it was flooding, the river would have been dangerous to cross, especially in haste. Instead, Morgan held his position and decided to face Tarleton when he arrived. Throughout much of the night, Morgan talked to his men, raising their spirits.

Tarleton had been pushing his men to the point of starvation and exhaustion, allowing them only a few hours of sleep each night. At 2:00, on the morning of January 17, Tarleton woke his men, ordering them to break camp and continue their pursuit of Morgan.

Morgan knew that, having set his men against the Broad and Pacolet Rivers, there was little chance for the green recruits to escape the coming battle.

Confident that Tarleton would push for a frontal assault, Morgan arranged his men into three lines. The first consisted of sharpshooters, some 150 by count. Next, about 300 militiamen. And last, close to 550 Continental regulars. He held the remainder of Morgan's men in reserve to flank Tarleton's forces as needed.

Right after dawn, Tarleton attacked with a frontal assault, sending 100 dragoons straight at the Americans. Morgan's sharpshooters cut them to shreds, forcing a hasty retreat. And the American sharpshooters had taken to mind to aim in particular at the British officers.

Tarleton then sent his infantry and focused on the flank of the American forces. One misunderstood order led to a retreat by the American third line, and Tarleton mistakenly thought he had the Americans on the run. But Morgan ordered the third line to turn and fire, in unison, at the advancing British.

Morgan's cavalry moved in to outflank Tarleton's now disorganized infantry. His second line moved in on Tarleton's other flank, creating a double envelope, frightening the infantry, and forcing nearly half of them to lay down their arms.

When the battle was over, Tarleton had escaped with roughly 200 of his men, 110 killed, 229 wounded, and 629 either captured or missing. The Americans suffered only 25 killed and 124 wounded.

THE NORTH CAROLINA CAMPAIGN

Great Britain's "Southern Strategy," after the severe losses and lackluster results farther north, was brilliant on paper but misguided in real life. South Carolina would not stay subdued, so Cornwallis felt he needed to take North Carolina to cut off the rebel supply lines.

First, take Georgia, then South Carolina, and work northward through North Carolina and finally Virginia. But the British successes in taking Savannah and Charles Town were rather hollow considering the profusion of Patriots throughout the southern backcountry. Like all tyrants before and after, the British craved order, and the Americans would not sit still long enough to receive it.

While Cornwallis strove to add North Carolina to the sequence of British gains, South Carolina was proving to be not the gain they had expected it to be. Patriots like Francis Marion were bedeviling British patrols and supply trains. Instead of a return to normalcy, the British lamented that South Carolina was "in an absolute state of rebellion."

After the disastrous British loss at Kings Mountain (October 7, 1780), the unexpectedly weak support from southern Loyalists dwindled to nothing. Cornwallis could no longer find Loyalists anxious to join his cause.

January 1781, Cornwallis moved into North Carolina, capturing Charlotte, but then suffered another blow at the Battle of Cowpens (January 17, 1781), a short distance to the west. Taking North Carolina thus became a grim necessity for Cornwallis. He needed to break the rebel spirit. The rebels in South Carolina were getting supplies and reinforcements from farther north, and he wanted to sever that connection. He also wanted desperately to capture or kill General Nathanael Greene and his men.

Two months after the Cowpens disaster, Cornwallis met

with Greene on March 15, 1781, at the Battle of Guilford Court House, several miles south of the Virginia border. In an hour and a half of bloodshed, Cornwallis won at a significant cost. At one point during the battle, Cornwallis ordered his men to fire grapeshot into the mass of soldiers, killing both American and British troops alike. Upon receiving news of the battle in England, parliamentarian critic Charles James Fox remarked, "Another such victory would ruin the British Army!"

At Guilford County, though the British had only 2,100 troops to the American's 4,500, the battle resulted in a British victory — of sorts, with the British suffering 93 killed, 408 wounded, and another 25 missing or made prisoners of war. On the American side, about 90 were killed, roughly 200 wounded who escaped, 75 wounded who were captured, and as many as 1,000 unaccounted for.

The long chase and the brutal victory had exhausted the British army. Because of his severe losses in manpower and the fatigue of his troops, Cornwallis retreated to the coast, to Wilmington, not far from the South Carolina border. There, he intended to resupply his forces. General Greene, whose forces remained largely intact, hounded the British retreat, then returned to South Carolina to continue reclaiming the state from the British.

While in Wilmington, Cornwallis received notice that forces under British Generals Benedict Arnold (the Patriot turned traitor) and William Phillips were on their way to Virginia. And while Cornwallis had thought to cut the supply lines to South Carolina by subduing North Carolina, it had become clear that he needed to cut the supply lines in Virginia to complete the work in North Carolina.

Whatever the soundness of his logic, Cornwallis favored joining forces with the other two British armies. After all, General Phillips was an old friend. For the moment, North

Carolina seemed hopeless. Thus, in April 1781, General Cornwallis moved his army across North Carolina once more and entered Virginia.

For the next two years, however, North Carolina remained in turmoil as Loyalists and Patriots fought each other, creating a statewide condition of civil war.

SUCCESS IN GEORGIA AND THE CAROLINAS

In the last three years of the war, 1781–1783, American Patriots reclaimed Georgia and the Carolinas for the cause of liberty.

Georgia was the youngest of the 13 former colonies, with a popular Royal Governor in the person of Sir James Wright (1716–1785). For these reasons, Georgia was the last territory to join the Patriot cause. Yet, Wright's popularity could not overcome the growing sentiment against British tyranny. In January 1776, Joseph Habersham led a group of Patriots with an arrest warrant to take the governor prisoner. A month later, Wright escaped and made his way to London.

After the British captured Savannah, Wright returned as governor only to leave again three years later, after the Yorktown surrender in late 1781. July 11, 1782, Sir James Wright returned to London, never again to see the Americas.

The Georgia Patriot government had been forced to flee to the South Carolina backcountry until Wright and the British abandoned Savannah.

Though the British held Savannah throughout the last few years of the war, Patriots continued to fight throughout the backcountry. Patriots attempted to capture St. Augustine, East Florida but failed. And while Patriots continued to make it difficult for the British to subdue Georgia, the few active Loyalists in the region made Patriot efforts more difficult.

By early 1781, though the British congratulated themselves on their successes in Georgia, the Patriot militia was quietly gathering resources to retake the Georgia hinterland. By April, American forces converged on Augusta, Georgia, and successfully claimed the town by the start of July. Though the British firmly held Savannah, Patriots and Loyalists continued fighting in the West.

One heroic Patriot named Nancy Hart (*c.* 1735–*c.* 1830) had immigrated to the lands west of Augusta before the war had started. A band of Loyalists visited her home in search of rebels, but Nancy shot two of them, captured the others, and, with the help of friends, had them hanged.

Meanwhile, General Nathanael Greene, after harassing General Cornwallis and his retreat to the coast in North Carolina, returned to South Carolina to restore the state to American control. Greene's successes frightened Georgia's Royal Governor Wright enough to have him beg for additional British regulars to ensure peace. However, Wright never received a reply.

In early 1782, General Greene took the Continental Army into Georgia after the Cornwallis surrendered at Yorktown to squeeze the British in Savannah into submission. This forced Governor Wright and the British military to abandon Savannah. More than a thousand Loyalists and their slaves evacuated with them.

General Greene then sent General "Mad" Anthony Wayne into Georgia to finish the task of eliminating what British forces remained in the southernmost state. Greene also sent a letter to Georgia militia leader General John Twiggs to aid General Wayne with as many men as he could spare from his work in the backcountry fighting Native Americans and Loyalists.

THE BATTLE OF THE CHESAPEAKE

In the most important naval battle of the war, on September 5, 1781, the French and British fleets met at the mouth of Chesapeake Bay.

General Cornwallis had fortified a deep-water position on the Virginia Peninsula on the York River. American and French forces closed in to lay siege against the British and to cut off any chance of escape by sea. The result was a major tactical win for the French in support of the Americans. The battered British fleet sailed back to New York for repairs and resupply.

The Battle of the Chesapeake was among history's most critical naval battles. Conflicts competing for this title include the Battle of Salamis (480 BC), pitting the Greek navy against the Persians, and the Spanish Armada (AD 1588) threat against the English. Each of these was pivotal in determining the broad sweep of future history. Western culture and philosophy may never have taken root without the brave Athenians in their smaller but faster ships. The British Empire may never have happened, and the English may speak Spanish today had it not been for a major hurricane just off the coast of England. But without the tactical win of the French fleet at the Battle of the Chesapeake, these United States and its history-changing Constitution may never have occurred.

CONTEXT: CORNWALLIS TO YORKTOWN

General Clinton, head of the entire British army in the Americas, had sent General Benedict Arnold (the American traitor) and General Phillips to Virginia — a state which, until then, had suffered only the occasional naval raid along the coast.

When General Cornwallis discovered that Phillips and Arnold were headed for Virginia, he decided to join them to cut off the supply lines to the South. So far, he had found it impossible in North Carolina. But when he arrived in Virginia, he discovered his old friend, Phillips, had died. Assuming full command of all three armies and receiving orders to fortify a deep-water port for establishing a stable line for British resupply, Cornwallis selected a point on the Virginia Peninsula adjacent to the York River at a small settlement called Yorktown. The location proved to be strategically weak unless British warships could find access. Cornwallis had his men fortify their position, awaiting the presence of the British fleet.

FRANCO-AMERICAN PLANS

During the summer of 1781, General Washington and French Commander comte de Rochambeau discussed where they should attack next. Washington desperately wanted to reclaim New York City, which he had lost in 1776. But the city was heavily fortified and would have proven costly in both lives and resources.

Rochambeau thought Yorktown would be a better target. French Admiral De Grasse had been in the West Indies since April. They contacted De Grasse and requested his help. On July 28, De Grasse sent a message to Washington informing him that he would sail for Chesapeake Bay on August 3 with between 25 and 29 ships.

FRENCH NAVY TO THE RESCUE

British Admiral Samuel Hood detected the movement of De Grasse's fleet. He headed north directly for Chesapeake Bay by a more direct route. His 14 ships of the line arrived at the

Bay on August 25 and, finding none of the French there, continued to New York City to join with Admiral Graves.

Also, on August 25, French Admiral De Barras left Newport, Rhode Island, heading south with a fleet of 7 ships carrying siege guns and other equipment which would be helpful in the attack on Yorktown.

When De Grasse arrived at the Bay on August 31, he had 27 ships. He sent three to the York River to block access to Yorktown while 24 waited for the British to arrive.

Five days later, their waiting was over. When the French spotted the British, De Grasse ordered his fleet to sea for more maneuvering room.

On the Franco-American side stood 24 ships of the line, with 19,000 sailors and 1,700 guns. The British had 19 ships of the line, with 13,000 sailors and 1,400 guns.

At about 4:30 in the afternoon, after hours of maneuvering, the battle began with the British shooting for the French hulls while the French aimed for the British masts. While both fleets suffered damage, the French strategy seemed more effective because the damaged British ships could not hold their positions because of a severe loss of maneuverability and power. After about two hours, the sun set, and both fleets broke off the engagement.

The French suffered 220 killed or wounded, and two ships were heavily damaged. In contrast, the British suffered 90 killed, 246 wounded, and five ships damaged, with an additional ship scuttled as beyond repair.

De Grasse led the British to sea, hoping to give De Barras time to arrive unscathed with his seven ships. Both fleets were in constant sight of one another. After four days, De Grasse abruptly left the British and returned to the Chesapeake to find that De Barras had arrived. Graves decided to return to New York for repairs and reinforcements.

THE YORKTOWN CAMPAIGN

Between September 28–October 19, 1781, the French and Americans laid siege to General Cornwallis at Yorktown. Cornwallis had selected Yorktown as a deep-water port to resupply the Southern Strategy. A larger French fleet from the Caribbean under Admiral De Grasse blocked entry into the Chesapeake, denying access to Yorktown. A smaller French fleet from Newport, Rhode Island, under Admiral De Barras, aided in the siege. The strategically poor selection of Yorktown led to the complete unraveling of the British Southern Strategy and a major American win. Though the war was not officially over, the Americans now had grounds to sue for peace — a peace that would give them the liberty they sought.

PRELIMINARY MOVES

In March 1781, after George Washington learned that Generals Phillips and Arnold had invaded his native Virginia, the American General sent Marquis de Lafayette to counter their moves.

When Cornwallis arrived in Virginia the following month, he took over his late friend's army. He continued to carry out his mission, raiding and destroying rebel targets. The combined forces under Cornwallis numbered 7,200, while those under Lafayette totaled 3,200. Because the French general had far fewer men, he decided against a direct attack but merely harassed the British army in their efforts. All the while, the Frenchman continued to accumulate more men. During this period, General Clinton, in New York, sent orders to Cornwallis, at first, confusing and some-times conflicting, but ultimately ordered his southern General to find a port for his heavy British warships so that their Southern Strategy could maintain a robust supply chain.

After selecting Yorktown, Cornwallis had his men build defensive fortifications around the community. Clinton's plan depended heavily on the ability to send ships to and from Yorktown. However, the French fleet under Admiral De Grasse foiled that strategy by giving the British navy a tactical defeat on September 5. With the French fleet blocking British access to Chesapeake Bay and the ships of Admiral De Barras moving in to assist in the siege on Yorktown, Cornwallis soon realized that he had become trapped.

SIEGE OF YORKTOWN

By late September 1781, General George Washington had all the men and supplies he needed to pressure Cornwallis.

Estimates of the men involved include 5,900 American regulars, 3,100 American militia, 8,800 French troops, and 29 French warships against 7,500 British troops and 1,500 German troops.

September 28, Washington moved his men out of nearby Williamsburg to encircle the British. The American commander-in-chief placed the French on the left side of Yorktown. In contrast, he placed the Americans on the right, which was the traditional position of honor.

Cornwallis had erected seven hastily-constructed redoubts and batteries connected by protective earthworks. He had also built batteries across the York River at a place called Gloucester Point to help protect the river.

After surveying his enemy, Washington determined that the British could be bombarded to the point of surrender.

Saturday, September 29, the Americans moved closer to Yorktown, which prompted British gunners to begin firing.

Though the firing continued throughout the day, there were only light casualties.

General Clinton had sent a message to Cornwallis promising an additional 5,000 men by October 6. Encouraged by this, Cornwallis tightened his lines by pulling all his men back from the outer defenses, except for the Fusilier's redoubt facing the French and redoubts 9 and 10 on the downriver side of Yorktown, facing the Americans.

The French and the Americans gladly moved closer to Yorktown by occupying the defenses Cornwallis had abandoned. Soon, they were establishing their artillery batteries at these closer locations. Trenches were deepened, and the earthworks otherwise improved.

Sunday, September 30, for two hours, the French attacked the Fusilier's redoubt but failed to take the British position.

Monday, October 1, the Americans and French learned from a few deserters of the British that their commanders had ordered the slaughter of hundreds of horses and had their carcasses deposited on the beach, all to conserve food.

Americans cut down thousands of trees to reinforce their earthworks with wood and began preparations for the coming siege. Setting up the French and American artillery was no easy task because the British kept firing their guns to disrupt their actions.

On Tuesday, October 2, the British stepped up the pace of their bombardments, killing several men. Despite the protests of his officers, General Washington made several visits to his front lines to assess the progress being made.

That night, British bombardments became a veritable storm in an attempt to cover for the transport of cavalry to Gloucester across the river to escort infantry on a mission to forage for food.

Wednesday, October 3, Lt. Colonel Banastre Tarleton led the foraging party and ran into the Virginia militia.

This forced Tarleton and his men to retreat, losing 50 soldiers.

Saturday night, October 6, allied troops began to dig the first siege parallel, despite stormy weather. The sky was overcast four days past the full moon, making it difficult for the British to see the massive digging project before them. Some 2,000 yards long, the French would command the western half, while the Americans would utilize the eastern half. Near the river at the French half, the allies dug another trench for gun emplacements for bombarding the British ships on the river.

Sunday, October 7, the British were surprised to see the new trench dug by the allies, every inch of it just outside the range of their muskets.

Throughout Sunday and Monday, the allies moved their guns into position, including three each of twenty-four and eighteen pounders, two eight-inch howitzers, and six mortars.

Tuesday, October 9, at 3:00 p.m., the French fired upon the British frigate HMS *Guadeloupe*, forcing it to move across the York River, where the British scuttled it to keep the allies from capturing it. By 5:00 p.m., the Americans had opened fire. Washington ordered that the barrage continue all night to keep the British from repairing what was damaged. British guns on the western side of town were silenced, and more British ships were damaged by the shells whizzing over the town into the harbor. Large numbers of British troops started to desert.

Wednesday, October 10, the allies spotted a large house in Yorktown. Thinking that the home may have been where Cornwallis stayed, the allies concentrated their fire on the structure, destroying it quickly. The French barrage on the harbor continued, setting the British HMS *Charon* on fire, a blaze that spread to two other ships.

In the Yorktown harbor, Cornwallis intentionally sank a dozen or more of his ships.

General Clinton informed Cornwallis that reinforcements would sail from New York on October 12. Still, Cornwallis stated in his reply that he doubted he could hold out for very long.

Thursday night, October 11, Washington ordered his men to create another parallel 400 yards closer to the British positions. This second parallel could not be extended to the river because British redoubts 9 and 10 blocked access. All night, the British continued to bombard the old line. By the following day, French and American troops had taken positions in the second parallel.

Sunday, October 14, Washington ordered all artillery within range to bombard British redoubts 9 and 10, both of which stood northeast of the allied second parallel. General Washington wanted to soften up both positions for a nighttime assault. The waning crescent moon would not rise until well past midnight, so the cover of darkness would be complete past twilight. Adding to that stealth element, Washington ordered that all soldiers wait to load their muskets until they had reached the appropriate redoubt.

Redoubt 9 was closest to the second parallel, holding 120 British and German troops. Redoubt 10 was adjacent to the river, containing only about 70 soldiers.

Starting at 6:30 p.m., the French attacked the Fusilier's redoubt on the west side of Yorktown, creating a diversion. All along the line, troop movements made British officers think that the Americans were preparing for an assault on the town itself. As darkness settled in, General Alexander Hamilton had his men fix bayonets to begin the assault on Redoubt 10. The Americans captured their prize, but the cost was nine dead and 25 wounded.

At the same time the Americans assaulted Redoubt 10,

the French advanced on Redoubt 9, quickly taking the fortified position from the Hessian troops guarding it.

Washington had his men move some artillery into the captured redoubts so shelling of the town could also be done from there.

Monday, October 15, Cornwallis focused all of his guns on the closest allied position, then had 350 of his troops storm the emplacements of cannons to disable the guns by driving an iron spike into their touch holes. They could disable six guns before the French drove them back to Yorktown. By morning all of the guns had been repaired.

Tuesday morning, October 16, even more allied guns were added to the line intensifying the barrage. Cornwallis became desperate, attempting to evacuate all his men across the York River. From Gloucester Point, he might have a chance to force his way through allied positions north of the York River and then move on to New York City. The first set of boats delivered their passengers. It returned for the next encounter when a squall made the crossing impossible.

From the British perspective, the Yorktown campaign had suddenly stopped.

Estimates of losses include 88 killed and 301 wounded on the Franco-American side, 309 killed, 595 wounded, and 7,685 captured on the British-German side.

BRITISH SURRENDER

On October 17, 1781, a drummer and British officer appeared out in the open with the officer waving a white handkerchief. All bombardments stopped while the temporary truce led to talks of surrender. During negotiations, Washington had Lafayette sit in for the French, insisting he be given the same authority as the American representative.

At first, the British requested the usual honors of war, but since the British had denied these to the Americans at the Battle of Charleston, Washington refused their request.

Finally, on October 19, 1781, the British surrendered to General George Washington and Commander De Rochambeau. On that humbling day of surrender, Cornwallis claimed to be ill. Instead of making a personal appearance, Cornwallis had Brigadier General Charles O'Hara deliver his sword to Washington. Similarly, Washington had General Benjamin Lincoln receive the sword of surrender on his behalf. We can only imagine Cornwallis's shame after his arrogance in treating the American rebels and the crime against his troops at Guilford Court House.

On that same day, October 19, 1781, the British fleet sailed from New York to return to the Chesapeake in support of Cornwallis, not knowing that the negotiations of surrender had begun two days earlier and were being concluded as the fleet set sail.

NEGOTIATING PEACE AND THE TREATY OF PARIS

During the final two years of the nearly nine-year war, Great Britain, France, Spain, the Dutch Republic, and these United States of America negotiated peace. General Cornwallis had surrendered at Yorktown in a miserable defeat for the British, and the remainder of the war elsewhere was not going well for the former motherland.

The Revolutionary War was not merely a local conflict but a global war involving five key nations. Negotiating peace was complicated because the Americans had agreed not to settle with Great Britain without French approval. This entangling alliance did not sit well with America's Founding Fathers, but they desperately needed French assistance.

After the surrender of General Lord Cornwallis on

October 19, 1781, peace negotiations took another two years before a treaty could be signed. Four sets of negotiations were to take place, each with its myriad details, but the American treaty, with French approval, would mark the beginning of official recognition by Britain, and other countries of the world, of these United States as a separate, sovereign nation.

Further complications came from territorial claims and counter-claims by each of the five main parties. For example, early informal British talks with Benjamin Franklin proposed that the 13 former colonies remain a part of the British Empire but with a degree of autonomy. This Franklin flatly rejected. Franklin wanted to include Canada as a part of liberated America, but the British rejected this idea.

The British were tired of war with these four other nations, but the French were desperate for peace. The war had taken them dangerously close to bankruptcy. Complicating the negotiations even further, France had agreed with Spain not to settle without its permission. Spain wanted to possess Gibraltar, at the southernmost tip of the Spanish-Portuguese (Iberian) peninsula. Such desire was a matter of Spanish pride. The British, however, saw possession of Gibraltar as their way of guaranteeing free and open trade with all the nations bordering the Mediterranean Sea. Spain and France had been bombarding Gibraltar for several years but with little or no effect.

Initially, Britain decided to cut their soaring costs by placing America on a "no offensive war policy." But France forced the British to move toward peace faster than some of the more hawkish members of Parliament were comfortable doing. In the Caribbean, the French were capturing one British island after another. This alone could have had dire economic consequences for the British Empire because each island of the West Indies produced great wealth for the English.

Still, Great Britain had sent their fleet to the West Indies to stop the losses in territory. Holding off on a settlement with the Americans might help them leverage a better deal overall.

The content of the negotiations included much more than merely liberty, sovereignty, and conquered lands; they also included reparations for Loyalists who had been deprived of their property and Americans who had had their property destroyed by a vindictive British army.

On October 10, 1782, Great Britain, with 33 ships of the line as escort, resupplied Gibraltar to hold out indefinitely against both the French and the Spanish. There was little chance the Spanish could force Great Britain to give up their Gibraltar prize.

November 30, 1782, a preliminary treaty was signed between the British and Americans, contingent on the French signing a similar treaty. France signed their preliminary treaty with the British on January 20, 1783. And finally, the American treaty was formally signed on September 3, 1783. However, the treaty was not official until it was ratified on January 14, 1784, by the Continental Congress, which at the time, was stationed at Annapolis, Maryland.

TEST YOUR UNDERSTANDING

Answers to the following questions may be found in the Appendix.

1. What error did Lt. Colonel Tarleton make which may have helped him lose at the Battle of Cowpens?

•He had not let his men rest adequately.

•He started the attack by having his men charge with fixed bayonets.

•He used the wrong type of musket.

•He attacked before letting his men set up their artillery.

2. What was the British General's strategic goal in North Carolina?

•To capture or kill General George Washington.

•To cut off the supply lines to rebels farther south.

•To give his boss, General Clinton, time to mount an offensive in the North.

•To establish a significant military port for supplying the British Southern Strategy.

3. After the initial battle near the mouth of Chesapeake Bay, why did the French Admiral move his fleet farther from the coast?

•To taunt the British with the French naval superiority.

•To give his own men time to repair their ships.

•To give the smaller fleet of De Barras a chance to reach the York River unmolested.

•To exhaust the British so they would be too tired to fight after their long voyage from New York.

4. What was the British general's chief mistake at Yorktown?

•The York River was not entirely "deep water" from the bay to Yorktown preventing the larger ships from having access.

•Cornwallis did not have his men dig their redoubts deeply enough.

•With his men starving, Cornwallis slaughtered their horses without considering using them as food.

•Choosing a location far from the open ocean where access from reinforcements and supply ships could be blocked.

5. What added to the complexity of negotiating for peace?

•The British insisted on taking Louisiana.

•The French desperately wanted to take Gibraltar from the Spanish.

•The British insisted on reparations for British property destroyed during the Revolution.

•The French had promised not to negotiate peace without obtaining Spanish permission.

SUMMING IT UP

Like their success at Kings Mountain, the Patriot win at the Battle of Cowpens had discouraged General Cornwallis even more about the British wins in their Southern Solution. Somehow, the rebels in Georgia and South Carolina were getting supplies and reinforcements, and he was determined to cut off that supply line. First, he tried to accomplish this in North Carolina. His desperation was revealed at Guilford Courthouse when he used artillery fire against his men to kill more of the Americans. Then, with General Clinton dispatching two armies to Virginia, Cornwallis decided to accomplish his aims in Virginia.

Though the Americans did not achieve major victories in Georgia and South Carolina after Cornwallis turned toward Virginia, their Patriot guerrilla tactics kept the British occupation guessing.

French ships came to the rescue when all eyes turned to Yorktown. The British hoped to establish a deep-water port to resupply their Southern Strategy. And the French navy kept the British from reaching their new supply port. Washington reluctantly agreed with his advisers to focus on Yorktown, even though he preferred reclaiming New York City.

Cornwallis had been promised fresh troops as reinforcements, but the French blockade prevented that. Foraging for food was made even more difficult because Yorktown was surrounded on three sides, while the hinterlands on the other side of the York River were patrolled by Virginia militia. With his men running out of food and resupply access blocked by the French, the British general realized he was trapped. And when a last-ditch effort to escape was thwarted by freak weather, Cornwallis was forced to surrender.

Negotiating peace after the world's second global conflict (the first being the Seven Years' War) proved highly problematic. Conflicting territorial claims demands for reparations, entangling alliances, and more forced negotiators into two long years of talks.

Once peace was achieved, the Americans could concentrate on living and creating a nation like no other in the long history of humanity.

A NEW NATION IS BORN

$\mathcal{H}$ow do you create a new nation? What form of government do you implement? What safeguards do you put into place to ensure the sustainability of such a young nation? These are some of the questions which no doubt crossed the minds of America's Founding Fathers. They had a blank slate and could write upon it anything they wished. But they were humble and fearful of the power they wielded. They had fought a long and hard war over the abuses of power and needed to guard against every conceivable abuse.

Each state enjoyed its measure of sovereignty and did not wish to become subject to a new tyrannical government.

One problem loomed over the young nation, threatening from the very start to derail their efforts: a massive war debt payable to France.

COSTS OF WAR

Wars are always expensive, not only in money but also in lost lives, infrastructure, and other harm.

FINANCIAL COSTS

In costs of money alone, the Revolutionary War created a burden of roughly 165 million pounds sterling (£165M). In a 2019 *USA Today* article, the estimated cost of the Revolutionary War in 2019 currency was $2.75 billion.

Because of the effect of printing large quantities of paper money, inflation skyrocketed, and the value of each Continental Congress dollar in circulation plummeted. Inflation led to the old saying, "not worth a continental," when discussing something considered worthless.

The largest single portion (39%) of that cost was paid with states' money, printed on paper. Another 28% was paid by money printed by Congress. But printing money with nothing supporting the value behind those dollars served to create inflation. People lost confidence in the paper.

For a while, the states and Congress could keep their currency afloat by selling off the confiscated property of Loyalists and by the gradual introduction of taxation. But taxation was one of the reasons for the war in the first place, so it was a sensitive issue. Most states put off taxation until the third year of the war.

Throughout the war, Congress printed close to $242 million.

Adding to the inflation problem, some counterfeiters started printing their own currency. And some counterfeiters were with the British military, hoping to weaken the American dollar even further.

Another 14% of the war costs were covered by states issuing Debt Certificates. Buyers could use their land as collateral and their principal with added interest after winning the war.

Congress covered another 10% by issuing their Debt Certificates but without added interest. They even used these to pay their troops, leaving virtually all soldiers dissatisfied with their payment.

Loans from Europe covered yet another 6%. After the win at Yorktown, America's representatives in Europe found it easier to secure additional loans to pay the Continental Army, which was active while peace negotiations were underway, and to make payments on the loan interest that had already come due. Once the British government had settled on peace with America, ironically, British investors were keen on profiting from loans to the young nation.

Though America had trouble paying back its loans — defaulting on scheduled payments to France in 1785 and 1787 — the new Constitution helped these United States finally settle their debts with the help of an American banker named James Swan. He bought the remaining French debt at a higher interest rate. Then he marketed those debt instruments in American financial markets for a profit.

And, last of all, 3% of the cost of the war was covered by Congress selling war bonds to wealthy Americans. While all investing comes with some risk, these bonds depended heavily on America winning the war.

COST IN LIVES LOST

The total cost in lives lost from the war was as follows:

American Cause:
- 6,800—United States
- 2,112—France
- 4,371—Spain

British Cause:
- 8,500—Great Britain
- 7,774—Germans
- 7,000—Loyalists
- 500—Native Americans

Approximate Total: Some 37,000 lives were lost due to the war. Many more lives were lost as an indirect result of the war through disease, poor conditions as prisoners of war, and other causes.

ADDITIONAL COSTS OF WAR

Wars destroy. Much more is lost than merely the lives of combatants and the financial drain on the economies of all nations concerned. Lost productivity and wages and lost infrastructure are included. But there is also an emotional toll from any such traumatic event.

THE LIMITS OF CONFEDERATION

As soon as the Second Continental Congress had appointed a team to write the *Declaration of Independence*, they turned their attention to creating a committee to produce the first Constitution of these United States. During the war years and the early of as a new nation at peace, the first American Constitution, known as the *Articles of Confederation*, governed the 13 former colonies. This first Constitution was the template for the American government. Because of some critical weaknesses, the Articles were replaced with the second Constitution in 1789.

While the *Declaration of Independence* acted to sever the relationship with Great Britain, the date of June 12, 1776, marks the first spark in the creation of a new nation and eventually pulled together the following representatives from the 13 sovereign states:

•Pennsylvania—John Dickinson (chairman)
•Connecticut—Roger Sherman
•Delaware—Thomas McKean
•Georgia—Button Gwinnett

- Maryland—Thomas Stone
- Massachusetts—Samuel Adams
- New Hampshire—Josiah Bartlett
- New Jersey—Francis Hopkinson
- New York—Robert R. Livingston
- North Carolina—Joseph Hewed
- Rhode Island—Stephen Hopkins
- South Carolina—Edward Rutledge
- Virginia—Thomas Nelson

MILESTONES OF THE ARTICLES OF CONFEDERATION

- Created: November 15, 1777
  - Ratified: February 2, 1781
  - Effective: March 1, 1781
  - Superseded: March 4, 1789, by the second Constitution

A UNION WHICH GOT THEM THROUGH THE WAR

Development of the *Articles* was started along with the *Declaration of Independence* because the Patriots knew they would require support from other nations, like France, and some form of Constitution would help the Americans look like a legitimate nation. A governance framework was needed to adequately wage the war that had started a little more than a year earlier.

July 12, 1776, only eight days after the *Declaration* was accepted, the first draft of the *Articles* was presented to Congress for discussion.

Finishing the Articles was not easy for the young nation during the war. After all, Congress had to move a couple of times, such as when the British took Philadelphia.

November 15, 1777, the Second Continental Congress

approved a draft of the *Articles* for distribution to the states for ratification. By February 1779, all states had ratified the *Articles of Confederation* except Maryland. Though the *Articles* were not official until unanimously passed, they were the *de facto* government throughout the remainder of the war. In other words, between February 1779 and February 1781, Congress and most states observed the *Articles* as their active Constitution.

Many philosophical debates on the second Constitution referenced specific clauses and their problems in the first Constitution. Thus, understanding America's current form of government depends on understanding the *Articles of Confederation*.

TURMOIL OF DEBT AND UNCERTAINTY

By the time of the *Constitution,* most people seemed to be against the *Article's* "Requisition System" of begging states for money. From 1782 to 1788, Congress would get between 22% and 48% of the requested money. This worked well to keep the central governing body from going crazy with spending. Still, it frequently fell short of its responsibilities, like paying war debts. The *Articles of Confederation* were simply inadequate to the fulfillment of the responsibilities of a central government.

However, Patrick Henry preferred requisitions to keep the central government constrained.

"**Requisitions, which gentlemen affect to despise, have nothing degrading in them. On this depends our political prosperity. I never will give up that *darling* word *requisi-tions;* my country [Virginia] may give it up; a majority may wrest it from me, but I will never give it up till my grave. . . . Requisitions are attended with one distinct**

advantage. They are attended by deliberation. They secure to the states the benefit of correcting oppressive errors. If our Assembly thought requisitions erroneous, if they thought the demand was too great, they might at least supplicate Congress to reconsider—that it was a little too much."

— PATRICK HENRY, JUNE 7, 1788, RATIFYING
CONVENTION.

But the Requisition System hampered the efficient operation of the government. Four broad areas were affected by the shortcomings of the *Articles*:
- A disorganized economy,
- A lack of coordinated guidance,
- Inefficient legislature, and
- Poor military protection.

A DISORGANIZED ECONOMY

Congress could not regulate trade, and the individual states were making a nightmarish mess of complex regulations. There was no standard currency, and each state printed its own dollars. The problems of inflation experienced during the war persisted. The central government's inability to get the funds needed to pay its debts was jeopardizing the future of America. Lenders would stop lending if the young nation defaulted too often on its loans. States grudgingly paid a share of what was needed but never 100% of what was required.

A LACK OF COORDINATED GUIDANCE

Foreign affairs were not adequately handled when 13 individual, sovereign states spoke with 13 separate voices. Also, there was no organized judiciary. There was no common judicial guidance for affairs affecting the nation. States ignored the edicts of the central government; this was too much freedom and not enough responsibility.

A severe lack of cooperation between the states significantly hampered the central government's ability to handle internal and external threats.

INEFFICIENT LEGISLATURE

On the surface, one vote per state may seem to be a good idea. But when some states had many more times the number of people than the least populous states, a small state could wield disproportionate power. Passing laws had become complicated because of the super-majority required to approve any legislation. And amending the *Articles* was nearly impossible because it needed unanimous support from all states.

POOR MILITARY PROTECTION

Each state had its militia to defend against foreign invaders, competing states, or an abusive central government. However, there were no adequate provisions for the common defense of the confederation. The Founders feared a standing army because they had seen what damage could be done by such a powerful organization. But 13 uncoordinated militias seemed inadequate to the threat of hostile nations. Indeed, the Revolution would have failed without the support and intervention of other nations, including the second-largest standing navy.

DEVELOPING THE SECOND CONSTITUTION OF THESE UNITED STATES

A new organizing structure was needed to overcome the deficits of the *Articles of Confederation*. Discussions at the Constitutional Convention of 1787 frequently referred to the *Articles* simply because this document was being replaced. The Founding Fathers needed to discuss what worked and what did not.

The Founding Fathers feared the misuse of power and sought to spread government power across many competing centers. They needed to add power to the "general government," but not too much. Under the *Articles*, the states were too powerful. Still, a powerful central government was precisely what they had fought in a long and bloody war to escape.

INITIALLY, the Constitutional Convention was held to discuss amendments to the *Articles of Confederation*. But the more the delegates talked about the *Articles*, the more some questioned the wisdom of its overall structure. They voiced a desire to start from scratch with a new constitution.

The convention occurred May 25–September 17, 1787, in Philadelphia. Delegates discussed competing plans, and James Madison's Virginia Plan won the most approval. Madison's plan provided a strong central government divided into three branches: legislative, executive, and judicial.

Besides adding an executive and a judicial branch, some delegates were concerned about sullying their new nation with the practice of slavery. One of the principles discussed involved states having representation in Congress in proportion to their population. But since slaves could not vote or own property, a concession called the "Three-Fifths Compromise" was made, where only 60% of the slaves were counted for representation purposes. The proponents of this measure saw it as an *anti-slavery* measure. Proponents did not want to give slave states more power to perpetuate slavery but wanted to reduce the power of "slave state" votes so that slavery could eventually be eliminated. Indeed, the purpose of the compromise was to ensure that slaves finally received 100% representation in Congress as fully-recognized citizens with the ability to vote and own property.

All delegates were sworn to secrecy so that each had the emotional and political freedom to discuss all ideas without fear of reproach from the public. As in the art of brainstorming, all ideas were welcomed. But once submitted, no idea was considered sacred except the underlying philosophy of a government that fulfills the needs of the people without unduly burdening the people.

Certain key principles guided them in developing a constitution, one of the primary being that governments exist by the consent of the governed. They knew that the individual's existence preceded all governments. Thus the individual was primary to all such discussions. Toward this end, the delegates sought to create a form of government that would protect the individual not only from the excesses of government power but the equal excesses of the majority, and by this, constraining the dangers of "democracy."

These Americans sought ways to diffuse the centers of power so they could not be easily abused.

"From the nature of man we may be sure, that those who have power in their hands will not give it up while they can retain

it. On the contrary we know they will always when they can rather increase it. . . . [t]he purse & the sword ought never to get into the same hands."

— *GEORGE MASON, PHILADELPHIA CONVENTION, 1787.*

Madison's Virginia Plan provided that the legislative branch would have the power of the purse and to declare war, while the executive would be commander in chief and lead in foreign policy.

However, the Founding Fathers also rejected the idea of giving people too much power, for a majority rule can destroy a minority; America's Constitutional Republic defended even the smallest minority—the individual.

"[A]n elective despotism was not the government we fought for; but one which should not only be founded on free principles, but in which the powers of government should be so divided and balanced . . . as that no one could transcend their legal limits without being effectually checked and restrained by the others."

— *JAMES MADISON, FEDERALIST PAPER #48, FEBRUARY 1, 1788.*

"It has been observed that a pure democracy if it were practicable would be the most perfect government. Experience has proved that no position is more false than this. The ancient democracies in which the people themselves deliberated never possessed one good feature of government. Their very character was tyranny; their figure deformity."

— *ALEXANDER HAMILTON, SPEECH IN NEW YORK, URGING RATIFICATION OF THE NEW U.S. CONSTITUTION, JUNE 21, 1788.*

Madison's Virginia Plan called for a two-chamber legislature (the Senate and the House of Representatives), both with proportional representation. William Paterson's alternative New Jersey Plan intended to give states equal representation in a one-chamber legislature. On July 16, 1787, the "Connecticut Compromise" merged the two plans, providing proportional representation in the House and equal representation in the Senate.

Not only diffusion of power but strict limitations on governmental power extended from the Constitution to the *Bill of Rights*. Before the war, if anyone were ever to write against the king, they risked prison. Enforced religious practice, like the state religions of past kingdoms, also concerned America's founders. Things like these led to the First Amendment to the Constitution.

When the British marched on Lexington and Concord in 1775, they had in mind not only arresting the leaders of the Massachusetts upstarts but in confiscating the arms held by their fellow rebels. This led to the Second Amendment.

Other abuses and the lessons of history also led to the provisions of the *Bill of Rights* and the Constitution itself.

Forcing colonists to house British soldiers was not only an inconvenience but also costly. Many also found it a traumatic experience after events like the Boston Massacre in 1770. The Third Amendment was inspired by such government overreach.

The British *"Writs of Assistance"* made Americans critically aware of the toxic nature of "general search warrants," which had given British soldiers the right to search and seize any property they deemed smuggled or illegal goods. Such parliamentary legislation was designed to assist the British in enforcing trade laws. These legal documents gave British authorities the right to enter, search, and seize warehouses, private homes, and ships whenever necessary. Not surprisingly, many British soldiers abused this power for personal gain. Boston lawyer James Otis, in 1761, fought for the colonists' rights in this matter but lost. His defeat only amplified the level of defiance amongst the Americans and ultimately led to the Fourth Amendment to the Constitution.

Thus, the American form of government became one where the "general government" (federal) had certain powers and duties beyond which it was not to venture. The Tenth Amendment was added to the *Bill of Rights* to remind the federal government that states, local governments, and the people retained rights and powers. However, the Constitution and Bill of Rights were far from complete. Even after both were ratified, serious problems remained, including the perpetuation of slavery, only some male citizens being allowed to vote, and women having no say in society.

AMERICA'S FIRST PRESIDENT

Some suggested that George Washington should be made America's first king, but the former commander-in-chief rejected the idea. Washington did, however, accept the responsibilities as America's first president.

George Washington was a national hero for leading the Continental Army to victory over the British. He had not been a perfect military leader but he ultimately prevailed. Washington was against forming political parties, for he felt they would lead to too many corrosive divisions that could tear the country apart. Though he had planned to serve only one term in office, he changed his mind when it became increasingly apparent that the nation needed a strong but restrained hand to guide its first few years of existence.

Washington's cabinet consisted of 6 men at a time, including himself:

•President George Washington—1789–1797

•Vice President John Adams—1789–1797
•Secretary of State:
•John Jay—1789–1790
•Thomas Jefferson—1790–1793
•Edmund Randolph—1794–1795
•Timothy Pickering—1795–1797
•Secretary of the Treasury:
•Alexander Hamilton—1789–1795
•Oliver Wilcott Jr.—1795–1797
•Secretary of War:
•Henry Knox—1789–1794
•Timothy Pickering—1795
•James McHenry—1796–1797
•Attorney General
•Edmund Randolph—1789–1794
•William Bradford—1794–1795
•Charles Lee—1795–1797

One concern held by Washington was the intense animosity between two of his cabinet members — Secretary of State Thomas Jefferson and Secretary of the Treasury Alexander Hamilton. Though Hamilton and Jefferson could agree on so much, their differences sparked great animosity, disrupting Washington's cabinet numerous times. One serious point of difference went to the heart of the inadequacies of the Articles of Confederation: debts.

"A national debt if it is not excessive will be to us a national blessing; it will be powerful cement of our union. It will also create a necessity for keeping up taxation to a degree which without being oppressive, will be a spur to industry . . . ."

— *ALEXANDER HAMILTON, LETTER TO ROBERT MORRIS, APRIL 30, 1781.*

'This exactly marks the difference between Colo. Hamilton's views and mine, that I would wish the debt paid tomorrow; he wishes it never to be paid, but always to be a thing wherewith to corrupt and manage the legislature.'

— *THOMAS JEFFERSON, LETTER TO GEORGE WASHINGTON, SEPTEMBER 9, 1792.*

THE TWO MEN continued to ignore their president's calls for calm cordiality. The philosophical differences between the two were so intense that each one created an opposing political party to organize support for their competing ideals. Hamilton formed the Federalist Party, while Jefferson formed the Republican Party, frequently referred to as the Jeffersonian Republicans. His party later changed its name to Democratic-Republican Party and then simply the Democratic Party. The modern Republican Party did not exist until the time of Abraham Lincoln, 62 years later.

Jefferson and James Madison wrote under pseudonyms for the *National Gazette* newspaper. Together, through this news outlet, they redefined the political landscape of the nation, which had only recently pitted those in favor of the federal government against those who were anti-federalists. Instead, they said the actual division was between the American "aristocrats" — a jab at Hamilton and his friends in the Federalist Party — and the Republicans.

Washington was swept into office in a landslide both times, in part because political parties did not exist (the first election) or were too new (the second election).

Throughout his two terms in office, Washington remained keenly aware that his actions would set a precedent for all future presidents. For instance, he established the proper form of address, not as "His Excellency, the President," but simply as "Mr. President." Also, he exercised extraordinary restraint in exercising the veto power, even if he disagreed with the presented legislation.

Washington never lived at the White House because it had not been built during his time in office. First, he occupied one of two different houses, in turn, both in New York City and then in Philadelphia. These held the national government until the main structures could be built in the new District of Columbia.

George Washington did not belong to any political party. He felt very strongly against the practice because he felt it would inevitably lead to the downfall of America. In his farewell address, he wrote,

> *"[Political Parties] serve always to distract the public councils and enfeeble the public administration. It agitates the community with ill founded jealousies and false alarms, kindles the animosity of one part against another, foments occasionally riot and insurrection. It opens the door to foreign influence and corruption, which find a facilitated access to the government itself through the channels of party passion."*
>
> — *GEORGE WASHINGTON, FAREWELL ADDRESS*
> *(SEPTEMBER 19, 1796).*

George Washington further warned current and future Americans against political parties—the factions which divide us even today.

> *"The alternate domination of one faction over another, sharpened by the spirit of revenge, natural to party dissension, which in different ages and countries has perpetrated the most horrid enormities, is a frightful despotism. But this leads at*

> *length to a more formal and permanent despotism. The disorders and miseries which result gradually incline the minds of men to seek security and repose in the absolute power of an individual, and sooner or later, the chief of some prevailing faction, more able or more fortunate than his competitors, turns this disposition to the purposes of his elevation, on the ruins of public liberty."*
>
> *— GEORGE WASHINGTON, FAREWELL ADDRESS*
> *(SEPTEMBER 19, 1796).*

IN CLOSING

One of the signers of the *Declaration of Independence*, physician Benjamin Rush declared, "[N]othing but the first act of the drama is closed. It remains yet to establish and perfect our new forms of government and to prepare the principles, morals, and manners of our citizens for these forms of government after they are established and brought to perfection." Franklin's prescient warning after the Constitutional Convention — "a republic, if you can keep it" — is as important now as it was back then.

TEST YOUR UNDERSTANDING

Answers to the following questions may be found in the Appendix.

1. What method was used by the young nation to help pay its war debts?

•Selling raffle tickets to the American rich and middle class.

•Selling part of the debt to an American banker who sold it at a higher interest rate.

•Amortizing the debt over the life of the country.

•All of the above.

2. What was a significant problem with the *Articles of Confederation?*

•America was unable to take care of its financial responsibilities.

•The term in office for the president was too short, giving them too little time to do anything constructive.

•The Supreme Court had too few members, thus raising the risk of partisan control.

•All of the above.

3. What was the original purpose of the Constitutional Convention?

•To discuss whether or not George Washington should be made king.

•To settle the philosophical differences between Thomas Jefferson and Alexander Hamilton.

•To write one or more amendments to the *Articles of Confederation*.

•To discuss whether or not the Supreme Court should have nine members.

4. What precedent did Washington set for the office of president of these United States?

•That the form of address should be simple and humble rather than grandiose.

•That the president should have term limits set at eight years in office.

•That the president should live away from the White House during part of his term.

•All of the above.

5. What problem was left unhandled by America's second Constitution?

•The inability of all American men to vote.

•The perpetuation of slavery.

•Disenfranchisement of women.

•All of the above.

SUMMING IT UP

Wars are always expensive, and those who profit from such things would like to be paid. Once the war was over, America, as a new nation, needed to face the costs of its enterprise. Part of America's early growing pains involved creativity in solving their vast war debt. And part of the solution was to scrap the *Articles of Confederation*, their first Constitution.

Though the *Articles* had been written to address many of the American colonies' problems under the British, the methods for solving those problems were far from perfect. At the Constitutional Convention, the delegates ultimately decided to abandon the *Articles* in favor of a new design for government.

The Founding Fathers feared power concentrated in the hands of a few or even in the hands of a majority. They sought to balance one center of power against another, hoping each could keep the other honest. Three branches of the federal government did this by taking on few but well-defined responsibilities—the executive branch, the legislature, and the judiciary. And even in the legislature, there were two parts—the house of the people and the senators who represented the states. Balanced against the federal government were the sovereign, individual states. Within each state, citizens had county and city power to balance against that wielded by the state. And finally, the individual citizens wielded their power to hold their public servants accountable.

APPENDIX

The following are answers to the "Test Your Understanding" quizzes at the end of each chapter:

UPRISING

1. **The Boston Tea Party**—Rebellious Americans dumped an entire shipment of British tea into Boston harbor on December 16, 1773, signaling their displeasure with the *Tea Act* (1773), which gave the British East India Company a monopoly on tea sales in the American colonies as well as their dissatisfaction with the *Revenue Act's* (one of the *Townshend Acts*) tax on tea.

2. **The French and Indian War**—In 1754, tensions between Great Britain and France were so high that conflicting claims over Ohio lands resulted in the military actions of Lt. Colonel George Washington triggering the American conflict, the French and Indian War (1754–1763) and this led

to the global conflict later known as the Seven Years' War (1756–1763).

3. **Declaratory Act of 1766**—This law meant to reassert Parliament's supremacy over the colonies, after the government repealed the *Stamp Act*, "to bind the colonies and people of America, subjects of the crown of Great Britain, in all cases whatsoever . . . ." The phrase "all cases whatsoever" was used as one of many arguments cited in the *Declaration of Independence*.

4. **Quartering Act (1765 and 1774)**—This law sought to force colonists to give shelter to the troops sent by Great Britain to enforce the unpopular laws Parliament had passed.

5. The Boston Massacre resulted in the death of 5 civilians after many in the crowd taunted British soldiers and threw objects at them.

WAR IS DECLARED

1. **United Colonies**—When hostilities broke out, the Americans still did not agree that they needed to separate from Great Britain. Some colonists still wanted to repair the relationship. At that point, they still considered themselves colonies of the Empire.

2. **Georgia**—As the youngest of the 13 original colonies and with the most significant percentage of recent immigrants loyal to the homeland, Georgia was the last to join the revolution.

3. **Because of his experience and ability to** unite people, George Washington was tested in battle

during the French and Indian War. Still, he also exhibited humility and restraint as a leader.

4. **To capture and destroy the munitions held there.**—Another critical reason British troops were sent to Concord was to arrest Samuel Adams and John Hancock, the rebellion's leaders.

5. **Just in case the British army increased their aggression.**—Tensions over the previous decade had escalated, making it likely they would continue to do so.

TURNING POINTS

1. **Unequal treatment of English citizens**—Most of the colonists still considered themselves to be Englishmen. Yet, those on the American continent did not enjoy the rights of their brothers on the home island.

2. The Americans had captured **Larger cannons from Ticonderoga**—Fort Ticonderoga only weeks earlier. Some of the guns had greater range than other armaments in the colonies.

3. **All of the above**—The British-appointed governors of the southern colonies had a vested interest in gaining military protection, so naturally, they would exaggerate the benefits gained by protecting their administrations. Regrettably, Loyalist support was not nearly as strong as they had hoped for the British. History is full of examples of a smaller force dominating the battlefield over a larger army, for example, the Spartans and allies holding off the far larger Persian force at the Battle of Thermopylae 480 BC.

4. **First Lieutenant Nathan Hale**—Nathan Hale was an American spy sent to investigate British forces during the fighting in the New York colony. He was caught and hung for his espionage efforts.

5. **Enlistments expiring**—The Continental Army regulars had hired on for a specific period that expired at the year's end. Washington needed their help in early January and asked them to extend their enlistments to handle the upcoming surprise attack.

STRUGGLES, SETBACKS, AND SUPPORT

1. **Foragers were in isolated groups far from the protection of their garrisons.**—General Washington had ordered his men to clear the land of as many forage items as possible. This would force the British to search farther from the protection of their garrisons, making them more vulnerable to attack and forcing them to spend more time for fewer rewards for their efforts.

2. **To split the colonies along the Hudson River Valley.**—This is an ancient tactic known as "Divide and Conquer." The most active rebellion had been in Massachusetts and New York. Splitting the colonies would prevent coordinated planning between the northern troublemakers and their friends in the larger colonies to the South.

3. **Alienating the citizens and creating more enemies of the crown.**—Any occupation will generate friction between the occupying force and the citizens whose territory is occupied. The British frequently took what they needed rather

than offering full compensation. And if an owner did not want the military to use their property, there was little they could do about it. During a prolonged stay, restless soldiers can abuse the citizens to alleviate their boredom.

4. **All of the above.**—General St. Leger lost his Native American support on his way to assist Burgoyne and was ultimately forced back by Patriot reinforcements. The support General Howe had half-heartedly promised was late leaving New York City. And Burgoyne lost the support of his Native American warriors.

5. **To the British military officers, the Americans were merely traitors and not enemy combatants.**—Because British command did not recognize these United States of America as a separate nation, the military action they took was one of putting down internal rebellion (treason) rather than defending against a sovereign enemy.

WAR GAINS PACE

1. **All of the above.**—Surviving the harsh winter in cramped quarters where disease could quickly spread was an accomplishment all on its own. When a team of 12,000 men is put to a singular task, they can accomplish great things, including building a new log cabin city to wait out the winter season. And Washington also set the task of learning professional military skills before his men.

2. **The French government would openly support the American cause for liberty.**—This was great

news, for it meant that all their sacrifices to date might lead to success. France had the second most powerful military in the world after the British. Combined with American zeal, Patriot hopes for their precious liberty seemed more than a little possible.

3. **He feared the French ships would cut off his supply lines by blockading the Delaware River.** —The British depended on their formidable fleet to deliver supplies and reinforcements. As an island nation, Great Britain depended on its navy more heavily than other nations. Besides, transporting supplies overland through enemy territory was too risky. Because of the geographical location of Philadelphia, direct access from the ocean was possible only through Delaware Bay and its chief tributary, the Delaware River.

4. **Molly Pitcher.**—At Monmouth, as the British returned to New York after abandoning Philadelphia, Molly Pitcher's husband manned one of the cannons. When he became injured, she put down her water pitcher and continued to fire her husband's cannon. "Molly Pitcher" is likely a nickname derived from her water-carrying duties.

5. **General Lincoln's men failed to stop Maitland's reinforcements from reaching Savannah.**—In support of the Patriots at Savannah, General Lincoln left Charles Town, South Carolina, and headed south with some of his men. He was to block access to the Georgia seaport to keep the British from receiving reinforcements. Those men failed to cover all possible paths.

REBELLION REVERBERATES

1. **To allow the Americans to surrender with the honors of war.**—This was, at the time, a tradition of competing armies in Europe, to allow the defeated army to surrender with dignity.

2. **Not listening to the advice of his officers.**—In any management position, whether it is in war or business, the leader is not all-knowing and needs to use the input of his trusted advisers before making a decision.

3. **All of the above.**—All these factors contributed to his betrayal. Benedict Arnold was a complicated man—industrious but vain. His second wife was half his age and the daughter of a Philadelphia Loyalist; she had also dated a British officer before General Clinton decided to abandon the American capital. Arnold was not going to pay off his debts on an officer's salary, and he had information that was extremely valuable to the enemy. If he had believed in the American cause the same way most Patriots did, no amount of money could have tarnished his sense of honor.

4. **After chasing Marion for hours, losing him in the swamp, Lieutenant Colonel Tarleton called him a "fox."**—The Carolinas have numerous swamps, and tracking an enemy through them can become next to impossible. The British have long been keen on hunting foxes because of the difficulty of the challenge. In a way, Tarleton was paying Marion a backhanded compliment by calling him a "fox."

5. **The soldiers on both sides were entirely militiamen.**—General Cornwallis had sent Major Ferguson to recruit more Loyalists to help fight the Americans. Because the British had captured the American upper-level command in the South, the planning and fighting had been left to the local militiamen and their leaders. The only British regular was Major Ferguson.

DAWN IS COMING

1. **He had not let his men rest adequately.**— Tarleton had been embarrassed too many times by these backward American colonials. He wanted to prove himself by capturing or killing the men he was chasing. Because of his impatience, Tarleton did not let his men sleep much. The night before their battle, the British Lt. Colonel had forced his men out of their bedding at 2 a.m.

2. **To cut off the supply lines to rebels farther south.**—Cornwallis had become increasingly frustrated with the American tenacity in their cause for liberty. The territory he gained would not stay conquered. The rebels in Georgia and South Carolina were getting supplies and reinforcements from farther north, and he wished to stop it.

3. **To give the smaller fleet of De Barras a chance to reach the York River unmolested.**—De Barras's seven ships carried siege guns and other equipment, which would prove very helpful to the Franco-American attack at Yorktown. If the British had seen the seven ships enter the

Chesapeake Bay, the British may have tried to stop De Barras and, by doing so, jeopardized the assault on Yorktown.

4. **Choosing a location far from the open ocean where access from reinforcements and supply ships could be blocked.**—General Clinton's mission for Cornwallis was to establish a readily accessible port to ensure supplies and reinforcements could make it to the British troops who needed them. Clinton's reason for abandoning Philadelphia was the exact reason for not choosing any location within the Chesapeake Bay. An enemy fleet could have blocked any port within the Chesapeake Bay at the mouth of the bay. A port on the York River could have been blocked by a fleet at the mouth of that river.

5. **The French had promised not to negotiate peace without obtaining Spanish permission.**—America's ability to end the war by suing for peace was hampered by the French requirement that the Patriots get their permission first. But the French would not likely give that permission until they received approval from the Spanish. And the Spanish were desperate to obtain Gibraltar from the British. After all, that rock at the southern tip of the Spanish peninsula was veritably surrounded by Spain. The presence of the British at Gibraltar was a thorn in their sides and a bruise to their egos.

A NEW NATION IS BORN

1. **Selling part of the debt to an American banker who sold it at a higher interest rate.**—Clever bankers can always think of new ways to make a profit. James Swan was at the right place at the right time to take advantage of that opportunity, helping America save face with the French, who had done so much to help them gain independence.

2. **America could not handle its financial responsibilities.**—Under the *Articles of Confederation,* the "general government" could only requisition state funds. There was no guarantee that the states would honor such requisitions. At most, the central government could only obtain 48% of the funds they requested.

3. **To write one or more amendments to the *Articles of Confederation.***—The delegates to the Constitutional Convention had felt that there were many things wrong with the *Articles* that a few well-designed amendments might fix. The more they talked about the problems, the more they realized the inherent flaws in the government's structure.

4. **That the form of address should be simple and humble rather than grandiose.**—Washington had made it clear that he did not want to be king. And during his presidency, he did not want to be treated as royalty. Instead of being called "highness" or "majesty" as with the monarchies of Europe, he asked that people merely refer to him

as "Mr. President," a custom which continues to this very day.

5. **All of the above.**—Originally, only landowners were allowed to vote, some thinking that other men were not sophisticated enough to understand government issues. Slavery was challenged with the Three-Fifths Compromise but was not resolved until the bloody Civil War over half a century later. Women were unable to vote until the early 20th century. Though America has improved on these issues, it remains a work in progress.

ABOUT THE AUTHOR

Eric Porterfield is a father, lawyer, professor, and author. He holds a B.A. in government and German from the University of Texas at Austin and law degrees from Baylor Law School (J.D., valedictorian) and Harvard Law School (LL.M.). He writes in the areas of law, legal education, government, and history.

Leave a Review

Eric Porterfield is an independent author and reviews determine, in large measure, whether this book is successful - or not. If you enjoyed this book, please leave your honest feedback. Eric reads every single review.

Made in the USA
Las Vegas, NV
05 August 2024

93415997R00105